BUILT TO FAIL

BUILT TO FAIL

THE INSIDE STORY OF
BLOCKBUSTER'S INEVITABLE BUST

ALAN PAYNE

LIONCREST
PUBLISHING

BUILT TO FAIL

The Inside Story of Blockbuster's Inevitable Bust

ISBN   978-1-5445-1777-3 *Hardcover*

978-1-5445-1776-6 *Paperback*

978-1-5445-1775-9 *Ebook*

CONTENTS

BLOCKBUSTER TIMELINE

Blockbuster passes on opportunity to buy Video Central, its largest direct competitor.

Hollywood Video, which has 15 stores, buys Video Central and goes public.

Wayne Huizenga buys controlling interest of Blockbuster for $18.5M.

Alan Payne leaves Video Central to manage group of Blockbuster franchise stores for Prime Cable.

1985   **1986**   **1987**   **1993**

David Cook opens first Blockbuster in Dallas, Texas.

H-E-B Grocery Co. opens first of 35 Video Central stores.

DVD introduced to
replace VHS tape.

Blockbuster opens 3,000th store.

Netflix is founded by Reed
Hastings and Marc Randolph.

Viacom buys Blockbuster for $8.4B.
Huizenga departs and Steve Berrard
becomes 2nd CEO.

John Antioco leaves Taco Bell to
become 4th Blockbuster CEO.

1994   **1996**   **1997**   **1999**

Hollywood Video
opens 500th store.

Hollywood Video
opens 1,600th store.

Blockbuster opens
5,000th store.

Blockbuster goes public
at $2.6B valuation, a 70%
decline from $8.4B Viacom
paid in 1994.

Bill Fields leaves
Walmart to become
3rd Blockbuster CEO.

BLOCKBUSTER TIMELINE

(continued)

Blockbuster opens 8,000th store.

Netflix has 2.5M by-mail subscribers.

Blockbuster launches DVD by-mail service to answer Netflix.

Netflix has 6M+ by-mail subscribers.

Redbox launches first major test.

Blockbuster by-mail has 3.5M subscribers.

2000 **2004** **2005** **2006** **2007**

Blockbuster passes on offer to buy Netflix for $50M.

Alan Payne founds Border Entertainment and buys Blockbuster franchise stores from Prime Cable.

Blockbuster ends late fees; stock price declines 50%.

Carl Icahn takes control of Board of Directors.

Netflix has 4M+ by-mail subscribers.

Blockbuster by-mail has 1.2M subscribers.

John Antioco resigns; Jim Keyes, former 7-Eleven CEO, becomes 5th Blockbuster CEO.

Netflix begins streaming movies.

Last Blockbuster
corporate store closes.

DISH Network
buys Blockbuster
at auction for
$320M.

50 franchise stores
still open. Border
Entertainment
owns 26 of them.

Ken Tisher still
running one
last store in
Bend, Oregon.

2010   2011   2013   2014   2018   2020

Netflix has 20M+
total subscribers
and market value
passes $10B.

DISH announces
remaining Blockbuster
stores will close.

Border
Entertainment
closes last store.

Redbox rents more
movies than Blockbuster.

Blockbuster files bankruptcy.

INTRODUCTION

Have you ever wondered why dominant companies fail? How seemingly invincible companies like Sears, Kmart, Kodak, Toys "R" Us, Borders, and dozens of others just go away? There is a long list, and when you think of the most memorable ones, Blockbuster is probably in your top five, especially if you are of the baby boomer generation. You probably spent a lot of time at Blockbuster. It was a weekly ritual with family and friends, a community gathering spot, and the beginning of the weekend.

Quentin Tarantino called the video store "...a cultural thing that was lost. And nothing worthwhile has taken its place. To tell you the truth, I don't know why it was lost."[1] After reading this book, you may wonder the same. Managed differently, could Blockbuster still be here today?

Blockbuster opened its first store in 1985, and in those early years, it was one of the fastest-growing companies of all time. From 1987 to 1994, it opened 3,000 stores, more than one a day—for *seven years*. It was led by one of the great entrepreneurs in U.S. history, H. Wayne Huizenga. He is best known as the only person to found three Fortune 500 companies: Waste Management, Blockbuster, and AutoNation. (Although Huizenga did not technically found Blockbuster, he bought it in its early stages and is responsible for building it into one of the most iconic brands in American business history.)

If you invested in Blockbuster stock when Huizenga was in charge, you did very, very well—even better than had you invested in Microsoft stock, which went public around the same time. Huizenga bought Blockbuster for $18.5 million; just nine years later, he sold it for $8.4 billion.

But if you invested in Blockbuster any time after 1994, when Huizenga left, you did not do well. You may have lost it all. Thousands did, including infamous corporate raider Carl Icahn, who calls Blockbuster, "The worst investment I ever made."

Why do you think Blockbuster failed? When I ask people that question, the answer is almost always "Netflix, of course." By Netflix, they mean the video streaming giant that is now the most valuable entertainment company in the world. Thousands of postmortem analyses of Blockbuster say the same. Even Netflix co-founder Reed Hastings recently attributed Blockbuster's demise to its inability to transition from DVD rentals to streaming. But that is *not* what happened. Blockbuster was in deep financial trouble long before Netflix ever streamed a movie.

So, if streaming didn't kill Blockbuster, what did? How can a company that so dominated an industry be in an almost constant struggle to survive? Because throughout its brief twenty-five-year history, the only thing Blockbuster ever did better than everyone else was open more stores. As the new home entertainment industry began to mature in the mid-1990s, Blockbuster's growth slowed, and competitors took dead aim. Opening more stores was no longer the answer, and Blockbuster was helpless.

TECHNOLOGY DID NOT KILL BLOCKBUSTER. BLOCKBUSTER KILLED BLOCKBUSTER!

The stories of failed companies are often told by their former leaders, whose main objective is to protect their own legacies. They sometimes acknowledge mistakes but more often cast themselves as victims of forces out of their control. The same is true of all Blockbuster CEOs. None have accepted responsibility for what happened. They blamed the company's demise on everything but themselves—predecessors, successors, bad movies, financial markets, uncooperative Hollywood studios, recessions, weather, anything but their own mistakes. But mistakes were made, and as you will discover, many were outright reckless.

This book is the comprehensive story of Blockbuster from start to finish, told by someone who was there the longest. You can find countless articles and academic studies about the company, and most of them are factual and informative. But when the writers attempt to draw conclusions about why Blockbuster failed, most of them get it wrong. Some horribly wrong. It is not intentional. They just "do not know what they do not know."

I ran video stores for 31 years, longer than just about anyone. The first six years were spent competing with Blockbuster when I ran operations for a chain of video superstores called Video Central. It was owned by the H-E-B Grocery Company, one of the most highly respected retail companies in the world. Our stores dominated Blockbuster, but I left when H-E-B decided to sell Video Central.

I spent the next 25 years as a Blockbuster franchisee and profitably ran our stores longer than anyone else—except for the very *last* store that still operates in Bend, Oregon. I saw it all and was on the receiving end of some of the most ill-advised business decisions imaginable. My company, Border Entertainment, survived years longer because we did not follow Blockbuster's lead and, in most cases, did the exact opposite.

Blockbuster was consistently outsmarted and outmanaged by smaller companies. And the challenges began earlier than you think—long before Netflix was even an idea in the minds of founders Reed Hastings and Marc Randolph.

Blockbuster was phenomenally successful in its early years and made thousands rich beyond their wildest dreams. But Wayne Huizenga built the company to grow and nothing else. And even though his successors had ample time to rescue Blockbuster from itself, we know that did not happen. Blockbuster became one of the most iconic brands in the history of American business, but it cracked at the first sign of a challenge. From its founding, Blockbuster was a company built to fail.

CHAPTER I

AMERICA GOES TO THE VIDEO STORE

"I say to you that the VCR is to the American film producer and the American public as the Boston strangler is to a woman home alone."

—JACK VALENTI, FORMER PRESIDENT OF THE
MOTION PICTURE ASSOCIATION OF AMERICA, IN
HIS 1982 TESTIMONY BEFORE CONGRESS

Yes, there was a time when you couldn't watch a movie or television show whenever or wherever you chose. Just forty years ago, the content producers (mostly Hollywood studios) controlled your viewing schedule. New movies were released only in theaters for limited runs, then taken away for years at a time before reemerging in repeat runs, or television where they appeared only in their designated time slots. The studios had complete control—that is, until the video cassette recorder (VCR) was introduced in 1975. And that meant war!

The VCR led to the creation of the video store and eventually Blockbuster. But, had the studios had their way, it would never have happened.

The studios believed copyright laws granted them complete control over their content, which included preventing citizens from recording programs on VCRs for private use. In 1976, led by Universal and Disney, the studios filed a lawsuit against the Sony Corporation to ban sales of its Betamax video recorder, and implicitly the VHS video recorder made by JVC. Remarkably, in 1981 (after there were already millions of VCRs in American homes), the Ninth Circuit Court of Appeals found in favor of the studios. Sony was, therefore, liable for copyright infringement by Betamax users. The lower court was ordered to impose an appropriate remedy, which included banning sales of the VCR. Hollywood had won.

But Sony continued the fight, and three years later, the case reached the United States Supreme Court, which, in 1984 and by the narrowest of margins, overruled the lower court in a 5-4 decision. The Betamax and the VCR were legal. Perhaps Fred Rogers' testimony (yes, *Mister* Rogers) tilted the case in favor of home recording when he defended it: "...I just feel that anything that allows a person to be more active in the control of his or her life in a healthy way is important." Thank you, Mister Rogers.

Surprisingly, during the court battles over the legality of the VCR, the studios began selling their movies on Betamax and VHS—to play on the very devices they were trying to outlaw. Trying to have it both ways, they began selling movies on video cassettes for retail prices up to $100. In 1977, Twentieth Century Fox was the first when they released *Patton* and *M*A*S*H*, which had been in theaters seven years prior, and *The Sound of Music*, which had its theatrical release in 1965. The first movies on videocassette weren't exactly new releases.

Given a family of four could watch a movie at the theater for about $15 in 1977, $100 for a videocassette of the same movie seemed outlandishly expensive. But from the studios' perspective, that was a fair price to *own* a movie versus the lower price to *rent* a seat in a theater to watch it. The price Fox set for these first releases became the standard for the industry. But even with the high price, thousands were sold, and the studio continued to release more and more—titles like *Butch Cassidy and the Sundance Kid*, *The French Connection*, *The King and I*, and many others. In fact, it was so successful, Fox bought the manufacturing company that was producing the tapes, Magnetic Video, less than a year later.

The remaining studios followed suit. Even Universal and Disney, which had filed the lawsuit to ban the VCR, joined the party in 1980, long before the case was settled. The dollars were too big to ignore. America was buying VHS and Betamax movies by the thousands. A new business was being created. But exactly who was buying them?

Most of these tapes were being purchased by electronics dealers, music stores, and other specialty retailers, but very few were actually *sold* through to customers because they balked at the high prices. That led to a few enterprising retailers who started to *rent* them instead. Hollywood never intended these movies to be rented, so they expanded their legal wars to a new front—outlaw renting. While still battling the courts to criminalize ownership of the VCR, they lobbied the United States Congress to outlaw renting movies on videocassette by way of the Consumer Video Sales Rental Act of 1983. But, by this time, the train had left the station. The fledgling video rental industry was already generating almost a billion dollars a year in sales, and growth was exploding. Congress did not have the stomach to pull the plug, and the Consumer Video Sales Rental Act never made it to a vote.

With all legal options exhausted, Hollywood had been dragged, kicking and screaming, into a new business. The VCR had been made to record television shows so they could be viewed at more convenient times. But when studios began releasing movies on videocassette at prices customers were unwilling to pay, an unintended consequence resulted. The video rental store was born. Thousands of video stores opened around the country, and retailers of all kinds joined the party—including supermarkets, convenience stores, and drug stores. Soon, this new video rental industry would become Hollywood's largest source of revenue.

In an attempt to bury the hatchet, Jack Valenti, President of the Motion Pictures Association of America, told the 1995 convention of the Video Software Dealers Association (VSDA): "TV did not kill radio or cinema, and we know that videocassettes didn't destroy movie attendance." Rather, he emphasized that videocassettes had *quadrupled* the amount of movie viewing in America.

Even Steven Spielberg, who had believed home video would take the magic out of movies, acquiesced. "I was wrong, thank god," he said. "Now, the video business and the motion picture business are a brotherhood forever. The buffer zone against failure has become the videocassette release, so thank you for that."[2] The business had come a *long* way.

Hollywood was unable to stop the creation of the video rental store, but through its pricing of movies, it imposed a business model that would play a pivotal role in the story of Blockbuster. You may be surprised to learn that video stores in those days paid about $65 for VHS movies. And several years of experience had taught video store owners that customers believed a fair price to rent one was about $3. This meant stores had to rent a movie 22 times just to recover its cost and many more times to pay expenses and generate a profit. The need to generate so many rentals during the high-demand period immediately after release made it impossible for video stores to stay in stock on all titles all the time. This created what years later was labeled "managed dissatisfaction." But it was not *mismanagement*, as some would later claim. It was an economic reality created by Hollywood's decision to charge video rental stores $65 for VHS movies.

This high price point dictated the business model of the early video stores of the 1980s. It drove a store owner's approach to everything from the initial investment to open a store to the cost of rent, utilities, insurance, taxes, labor, and everything in between. And it did not materially change until the late 1990s when the digital video disc (DVD) was introduced. That was a revolutionary change that transformed the industry, and one that will be explored in detail in Chapter 7.

The high price also led video stores to require that movies be returned within a designated time period—usually one or two days. A movie sitting atop a television set in a customer's home was not just collecting dust. It was also collecting *late fees*, which stores charged so customers would return it on time so it could be rented again. The heaviest demand for movies lasted only a few weeks after release—just like in theaters—so keeping those videocassettes rented during that critical time was mandatory. Otherwise, a store would not recover its cost and would not be in business for long. If there was another way to encourage the timely return of movies, no one ever discovered it. Late fees became a part of the video rental store business model, the same as any rental business—Avis Car Rental, for example. Years later, late fees would play a critical role in Blockbuster's demise, a sad story told in Chapter 9.

Hollywood occasionally released lower-priced VHS movies they intended to sell directly to consumers. These were usually big box-office movies studios believed more people preferred to *own* than rent. The retail price of these releases was about $25, and they became known as "sell-through" titles. The press often reported that video stores were not allowed to purchase these titles at sell-through prices and were forced to pay the $65 price for what had become known as "rental" titles. That was never the case. Video stores bought these titles at a wholesale cost of about $18, and, with rare exception, they rented more than they sold—and were very profitable. This learning played a critical role as the business transitioned to DVD when *all* titles were priced at about $18.

While almost all movies that targeted adults rented more than they sold, this was definitely not the case for those made for kids. Walt Disney Studios capitalized on this segment of the business with spectacular success. After experimenting with some lesser-known titles, it released the classic *Cinderella* in 1988 at a retail price of $29.95. It sold 6 million copies and generated $180 million in revenue, almost as much as Disney believed its entire catalog to be worth![3] But that was just the beginning. As VCR ownership grew, so did sales of Disney movies, the largest of which was *The Lion King*, which in 1995 sold a mind-boggling 32 million videos and generated over a half-billion dollars in sales! Through the mining of its classic movies in addition to new productions like *Aladdin*, *Beauty and the Beast*, and many others, Disney became the king of home video. But the business became a goldmine for *all* the Hollywood studios. By 1987, sales of VHS cassettes had become its largest source of revenue—the business it tried to kill before it even started.

The success of video stores led to an orderly release of new movies to VHS videocassette. Like clockwork, movies were released to video every Tuesday about six months after their theatrical release. Lines of customers waiting outside stores to rent the new release of the week became commonplace. Many wanted to re-watch movies they had already seen in theaters, and others rented movies for which they had chosen to "wait for the video."

And as the studios released more of their back catalog, a massive collection of older movies could be found in the progressive video rental stores of the 1980s. For the first time ever, customers could watch a favorite like *Gone with the Wind* or *Casablanca* as many times as they chose. No longer did they have to wait for studios to air them on television, complete with dozens of commercials. As years passed, thousands of these movies were released on VHS videocassette.

The video rental industry also launched and funded an unprecedented independent film movement. Films that previously would have never been made found an enthusiastic audience in the video store. As Quentin Tarantino put it: "From 1988 to 1992, people [movie producers] were all of a sudden getting $800,000 or $1 million or $1.2 million to make their little genre movie."[4] Tarantino's first film, *Reservoir Dogs*, was released in 1992 and is considered by many to be the best independent film ever made. It was produced on a shoestring budget for just $1.5 million and may have never been made without the built-in customer base provided by video rental stores.

In many ways, those early video stores were a more convenient destination for customers than the fragmented streaming services of today. Video stores had become the *chief aggregator of movies*. They had *all* of them. Today, one would have to subscribe to multiple streaming services to gain access to a similar amount. In the golden age of the video rental store, customers could find just about any movie they were looking for—all in one place and at a fraction of the prices of today.

So, it should not be surprising that as the studios became full converts to this new way to watch movies, the business exploded and experienced over 20 percent annual growth throughout the 1980s and early 1990s. The business became so big, it alone was covering almost all of Hollywood's production, distribution, and marketing costs—for all its movies. And for the most part, sales had been incremental, having not cannibalized Hollywood's other businesses—most importantly, theaters. This provided the "buffer zone against failure" to which Steven Spielberg referred. In many cases, theatrical releases did not recover costs, but shortfalls were always made up in the video release. Production budgets exploded, and with it came even bigger box-office movies, as well as thousands of smaller productions that would have never been made without the "buffer zone."

Home video had become the golden goose to studios, one which no one could have imagined just a few years earlier. It had completely transformed a business from one that had tightly controlled access to a few movies into one of total abundance. The market for Hollywood's movies was larger than anyone could have imagined, and video rental had led the way.

By 1987, thousands of video stores around the country were generating over $3 billion a year in sales. The business had been created by entrepreneurs who wanted their share of this exploding business, and many could be definitively described as "mom-and-pops." Instead of attracting retail professionals, the early video store owners came from all sorts of backgrounds and wanted in on the party.

In many cases, the business attracted real estate professionals who learned of it from their video store tenants. One of these was Bob Wenner, who opened a small video store in Dallas, Texas, in the mid-1980s. He named it *Video Schmideo* and boasted that it made money from the day he opened the doors until he sold it a few years later. "It wasn't that hard!" he proclaimed. Like so many of those early video store owners, Wenner came to love the business and later managed real estate and legal for one of the largest Blockbuster franchise groups in the country.

As the business grew at a frenetic pace, chains of stores began to develop. Video Station (which could trace its roots to the very first stores) was the largest with about 500 stores. Others such as National Video, Adventureland Video, Erol's, Video Concepts, and Video Biz all had more than 100 stores. But none of these chains could keep up, and every one of them would fail in the next few years. These pioneers and thousands like them had built the industry, but most did not fully understand its potential and were ill-prepared to deal with what was to come.

Most of the early video stores were in secondary locations, were too small, dimly lit, and not particularly well-managed. Many had X-rated movies in back rooms, and some even had private "viewing rooms." Most managed their inventories manually, having not taken advantage of the new personal computers of the day. Only a handful of video store owners had attempted to take the business to the next level, and even those who had were not prepared for what would happen next.

It was 1987, and a garbage man from Florida was about to take over the industry.

CHAPTER 2

BLOCKBUSTER TAKES CHARGE

"This is an industry with an image problem, a fragmented industry of dimly lit stores and X-rated movies."

—WAYNE HUIZENGA IN 1988, CHAIRMAN
OF BLOCKBUSTER, INC. 1986-1994

What is the connection between Blockbuster, the dominant force in home entertainment for over 20 years, and Waste Management, the largest garbage company in the world? H. Wayne Huizenga. He founded Waste Management in 1971, and although he did not *found* Blockbuster, he bought controlling interest of the company in 1986 when it had only twenty stores. He and two partners from Waste Management paid $18.5 million for 60 percent of the company, and Huizenga became its Chairman and CEO. Eight years later, in 1994, Huizenga sold Blockbuster to Viacom, Inc. for $8.4 billion, by far the most it was ever worth.

Huizenga is the only person in history to have built three Fortune 500 companies. In addition to Waste Management and Blockbuster, he also built AutoNation into the largest car dealership in the country—in just three years. Two of those companies still lead their respective industries. Blockbuster, arguably the most iconic of the three, is gone.

Huizenga was a self-made billionaire. He founded his first garbage company in 1962 with a $5,000 loan from his father-in-law to buy one truck and some routes in Broward County, Florida. In fact, it was the only company he ever started from scratch. Every other one, hundreds of them, he bought. And his primary way to grow those companies was to buy more. After taking Waste Management public in 1971, he bought 133 waste companies—in just 10 months. Just one day after he took control of Blockbuster in 1986, he was on the road to buy its largest competitor, Major Video—and he did.

Wayne Huizenga was all about buying, building, and selling companies. He often said that he was much more interested in building them than running them. The day-to-day grind of running a business did not inspire him. As Don Flynn, Huizenga's Chief Financial Officer at Waste Management, would describe him: "I think Wayne always wanted to grow faster and Dean [his partner Dean Buntrock] was more concerned with, 'Can we manage it?' Whereas Wayne would rather buy it, then figure out how to manage it."[5] Buntrock agreed: "Wayne is motivated by money and unbelievable financial success, but he is much more motivated by the hunt, the excitement."[6]

In the case of Blockbuster, the entire organization took on Huizenga's approach to business. It was obsessed with growth and little else. It was the company's reason for existence and, in just a few years, thousands became rich as Blockbuster grew from 20 stores to over 3,000. But it was this singular focus on growth that also led to Blockbuster's downfall. When competition came knocking, which was sooner than you think, they were lost. If they couldn't buy it or overpower it with even more stores, they struggled mightily to find answers. Growth, at whatever cost, became so much a part of Blockbuster's DNA that it carried over to Huizenga's successors and persisted long after he was gone.

Huizenga ran Waste Management with his partner Dean Buntrock for 12 years and left in 1983. After taking a few weeks off, he proceeded to do what he knew best—buy businesses, lots of businesses. Through his new company, Huizenga Holdings, and with the assistance of his new business associate, Steve Berrard, he went on a buying spree. They bought bottled water companies, a portable toilet company, lawn care companies, pest control companies, and many others. In three years, they bought more than 100 businesses. All of them were service companies and most *rented* things. Even the bottled water company was a rental company in those days with its dispensers for the five-gallon jugs delivered every week. All had similarities to the garbage business, which essentially *rented* waste containers to be serviced by a fleet of trucks.

Huizenga planned to roll these companies into one giant service company and go public, which would have given him the financial clout to grow even faster. Blockbuster or anything like it was nowhere in his plans, but perhaps it was inevitable. Blockbuster was, after all, a rental company like all the others he had bought, and its first franchisee, Scott Beck, was the son of Waste Management Co-founder Larry Beck. And it was John Melk, also a past associate at Waste Management, who persuaded Huizenga to look at a Chicago Blockbuster store in 1985.

Huizenga was attracted to Blockbuster for the same reason as most other video store owners. When run right, video stores were incredibly profitable—from the day the doors opened. "Hell, if the numbers are half this good, it's worth a look," he told his business associates.[7] Every successful video store owner of the day had discovered a once-in-a-lifetime opportunity, and thousands took full advantage. But *no one* had the vision or the financial skills to do it the way Huizenga did it—the same way he had done it with Waste Management.

David Cook, who founded Blockbuster, had opened the first store in Dallas, Texas, on October 19, 1985, about eighteen months before Huizenga visited that store in Chicago. But his path to the video business was an unusual one. He had founded Cook Data Services, a company that mainly supplied computer software to oil companies and raised $8 million when he took it public in 1983. But, within weeks of the IPO, OPEC announced it was slashing prices to maintain its stranglehold on the world oil market. The impact on the U.S. oil business was devastating, and Cook lost most of his clients. Faced with disgruntled shareholders, he searched for other ways to deploy the recently raised capital, and, in an unlikely twist of fate, the loss of his oil company clients led to the creation of Blockbuster.

Cook's ex-wife Sandy initially raised the idea of opening a video store and believed it needed to be bigger and brighter than the typical store of the day. She went on to design the famous torn ticket logo, as well as the store décor with its bright lights and soon-to-be iconic blue and gold color scheme.

The store was an immediate, runaway success. "The first night we were so mobbed we had to lock the doors to prevent more people from coming in," recalls Cook.[8] Blockbuster stores were a game changer. These bright, beautiful stores were in high-traffic, easy-to-access locations and attracted thousands of customers—many of whom had never been inside a video store. Cook had indeed created a *blockbuster,* and Cook Data Services soon became the Blockbuster Entertainment Corporation.

Cook planned to roll out hundreds of stores across the country. "Before we even opened our first store," he said, "we had spent $6 million to create a national distribution center in Dallas."[9] He sold Blockbuster licensing rights to developers and planned to have 1,000 stores open in three to five years. The distribution center would ship what Cook called a "store in a box" to the licensees. Included were inventory, fixtures, a computer system, even the toilet paper for the restrooms. The distribution center was designed to load as many as three stores in one day. Cook's sales message to potential licensees was: "Unload the truck, and you're in business!"[10]

With the infrastructure built and big expansion plans, Cook returned to the capital markets for more money to finance the growth. A secondary offering was scheduled to raise another $18 million, but what followed was a precursor to what would plague the video rental business for years to come. In a scathing commentary, the September 1986 edition of *Barron's* questioned the viability of Cook's plan, essentially claiming that anyone could do what he was doing. Blockbuster Entertainment was the first video rental company to go public, and Wall Street did not understand it, believing it was a scam that would have a very short life. Because the business was so profitable, it seemed "too good to be true" to many.

The *Barron's* article caused Blockbuster stock to drop, and the secondary offering sank from planned proceeds of $18 million to only $4 million. "The *Barron's* story was the single changing point in my life," Cook would say.[11] With the washout of the planned secondary public offering, he sought money from other sources to fulfill his growth plans and soon sold controlling interest to Huizenga and his two partners, John Melk and Don Flynn, both of whom were former associates at Waste Management. Huizenga assumed the role of Chairman and CEO, and Cook sold his stock and left with about $20 million. "I'm clearly not the best manager in the world for a large corporation," Cook said years later, who openly admits he did not see it that way then. "I haven't found anybody who doesn't think Blockbuster did a lot better under Wayne—including me." Cook said he sacrificed about $300 million by not holding on to his stock for a few more years (Hyatt 2003).

Huizenga was now in charge of a cash machine. Almost all the first Blockbuster stores were generating more than $1 million in annual sales, and remarkably, about a third of that fell to the bottom line—$300,000+. The first stores cost about $500,000 to open, which was usually repaid in less than two years. And year after year, the stores grew, every year making more money than the last.

Remarkably, every store was cash flow positive from the moment the doors opened for business. There was no long ramp-up to build a profitable base of customers. The pent-up demand for video rental was so high, the money came instantly. As each store opened, cash was produced to open another, and another, and another...

But organic growth was not fast enough for Huizenga. Staying true to his Waste Management strategy, he bought hundreds of competitors, almost always with company stock to preserve cash. Sometimes he bought them to convert to a Blockbuster store, and other times to close them, which would push more sales to nearby Blockbuster stores. To accelerate growth, he sold franchises for areas of the country he couldn't develop fast enough. But because he would never allow Blockbuster to be a franchise-driven company, he soon bought back most of the larger ones. Franchise stores never exceeded 25 percent of the total store base and thus never had much say in how the company was run. This was in direct contrast to most franchise companies, like McDonald's, for example, where almost all stores are independently owned by franchisees.

Over the next few years, Huizenga would bring legitimacy to the video rental industry. Although he would have many battles with Wall Street over accounting rules and threats from technology, he also had his share of believers. In six years, Blockbuster stock increased 100 times after Huizenga took charge. Every dollar invested was worth $100 by 1993!

Huizenga brought credibility to the video business and opened the capital markets to several other upstart video rental chains that would expand in the coming years. But none could move as fast as Huizenga—not even close. His vision of "how big was big" was foreign to everyone else in the industry. But despite the spectacular success of the early Blockbuster stores, they weren't doing anything that others couldn't easily do. What he had built was arguably the "best in class" at the time, but Huizenga recognized they were vulnerable. "We have to move fast because we have nothing exclusive...anybody can duplicate this," he said.[12]

Huizenga knew he needed to move fast, even faster than he had at Waste Management and his other companies, but he also knew he was not a retailer. Although Blockbuster was a rental company like hundreds of others he had owned, it was unlike anything Huizenga had ever managed. Blockbuster had storefronts and everyday face-to-face engagement with customers who could switch to a competitor across the street at any moment, nothing like garbage customers who were often under contract. And perhaps more than anything else, Blockbuster was in the entertainment business. It bought almost all of its product from a small group of notoriously fickle Hollywood studios, who would forever remain skeptical of the industry they had tried so hard to kill. Buying movies had nothing in common with buying trucks and dumpsters.

So, to shore up his team, Huizenga sought experienced retail managers to execute his plans. He hired several, but the most notable were Luigi Salvaneschi and Tom Gruber, both of whom had spent several years at McDonald's in real estate and marketing, respectively. Salvaneschi would serve as president in those early years and was charged with building the real estate and operating teams to roll out stores at lightning speed. Gruber built the Blockbuster brand, which, in just a few short years, became synonymous with the video rental business.

Blockbuster's two taglines saturated the airwaves during those first years, *"Wow! What a Difference!"* and *"America's Family Video Store."* Both were simple, straightforward statements to differentiate Blockbuster from the thousands of smaller, darker stores all over the country. With rare exception, Blockbuster really *was* different, and it never carried X-rated movies like many other stores. Gruber grew the annual marketing budget from just $5 million to over $100 million in less than five years and solidified Blockbuster as the *only* national brand in the industry.

The primary mission of Huizenga's newly assembled retail management team was growing, and they were compensated commensurately. Most took pay cuts from former jobs in exchange for lucrative stock options, which would be valuable only if the company grew. And grow it did. Within two years, Blockbuster grew from a few dozen stores to over a thousand, and then opened 2,000 more in just three years. Single-handedly, they would grow the entire video rental industry by over 50 percent in just five years.

The newly assembled retail team was essential to the success of Blockbuster. But none were a part of Huizenga's inner circle, which was often termed "Friends of Wayne." This was reserved for Co-founders John Melk and Don Flynn, right-hand man and financial guru Steve Berrard, and a handful of others, including Bob Guerin, the head of franchising. None of the "Friends of Wayne" had any experience with retail companies, and, in fact, the decision-making circle was even tighter. Berrard often said that all of Blockbuster's decisions were made by a committee of two—he and Huizenga—and only one vote counted.

As time passed, it became apparent that deal-making and the "thrill of the hunt" drove this group's thinking more than anything else. The day-to-day grind-it-out, competitive nature of most successful retailers was not a characteristic of the "Friends of Wayne." This soon became a liability that would be fully exposed.

Salvaneschi said as much in his last meeting with the board of directors before he left in 1992. "I think this company is too much development and financially oriented, and I think the customers are suffering, and you need to put more emphasis on the operating of the stores."[13] But Huizenga and his inner circle never got the message. Because of their approach to business, it is likely they had no idea what Salvaneschi was talking about. They had opened 3,000 stores, taken over an industry, and all made millions. Where was the problem?

The liabilities created by Huizenga's growth-at-all-costs strategy were first revealed in its deficient management information systems. When Blockbuster's first store opened in 1985, their computer system was state-of-the-art, but technology was moving at astonishing speed. When Berrard requested money to upgrade systems to better manage the inventory, Huizenga rejected the requests. "...give me a better solution than tell me I've got to sacrifice building 40 [new] stores for some goddamn systems for you damn accountants. I don't need damn systems to tell me we have too many tapes in the stores. Just go in on Saturday night. If the damn things aren't rented, then obviously you have too damn many of them!" For a time, that's exactly what stores did. They counted tapes on Saturday nights and reported them on Monday mornings.[14]

That exchange with Berrard is a window into how Huizenga viewed the business. For all of his genius in marshaling the resources to grow Blockbuster, he simply did not care much about how the stores operated, so long as they were open and generating fabulous sales and profits. The underlying details of how that happened did not interest Huizenga, and that behavior permeated the entire company. Phenomenal success had been achieved by building stores faster than anyone else. But the company's lack of curiosity about what went on in the stores, as well as competitors' stores, left gaping holes in its understanding of the business. And there is no better example of that than its management, or lack thereof, of its massive movie database.

Blockbuster had accumulated more data on the movie viewing habits of Americans than any company in history. Its CEOs often boasted about this massive database, and they were right. If you rented from Blockbuster, they knew almost as much about you as your banker. They knew every customer's gender, age, address, and every movie they ever rented—hundreds of millions of them. The Hollywood studios had nothing close to this level of detail. Their knowledge was limited to what they learned at pre-release screenings and small surveys conducted at theaters. Blockbuster was sitting on a gold mine of information, but what would they do with it?

Blockbuster's early years ran concurrently with the explosive growth of computer technology that made data management efficient and economical. (Microsoft, for example, went public the same year as Blockbuster.) But Huizenga's comment about counting tapes on the wall was only a slight overstatement of how the company collected and managed data. As computer technology marched forward, Blockbuster was left behind, long before movies via the internet were a factor. During its entire 29-year history, the store computer systems and back-office management systems were never significantly upgraded.

Blockbuster could have and should have understood the movie business better than anyone. But we know that was never the case because competitors saw what was coming before they did—every time. With its massive database to use as the ultimate guide to the future, Blockbuster should have *led* the way with its own ideas. But instead, they *followed* the path created by others with old, tired answers—and were always too late.

By 1992, just six years after Huizenga took control of Blockbuster, the company dominated the industry and was generating more cash than it could spend opening new stores. "We can't build enough stores to spend all this money, so what are we going to do with it?" Huizenga would ask. "We can pay higher dividends, buy back shares, or grow this business. We're the kind of guys who want to build something."[15]

Blockbuster was at a crossroads. It could have taken a breath and considered the inevitable mistakes made while in hypergrowth mode. Or it could have used the money to expand its empire by buying other businesses. Or it could have done both. But with Huizenga in charge and a $1 billion pile of cash burning a hole in his pocket, there was never a doubt what would happen next. Instead of investing in the stores to make them better, Huizenga did what he did best: *buy things*, with the goal of transforming Blockbuster from a video rental company into an entertainment conglomerate.

Huizenga bought 500 music stores under multiple brands believing he could "Blockbusterize" a mature industry run by longtime veterans. He even did a joint venture with Richard Branson, who was developing Virgin Megastores, which had music, movies, and everything related. Berrard confidently proclaimed: "We're going to change how this industry operates."[16] But even though the music business was in a time of unprecedented growth due to the success of the compact disc, Blockbuster Music failed in spectacular fashion. If there ever was a business that required a deep understanding of the limitless tastes of its customers, it was the music business. Blockbuster never demonstrated the ability to fully understand its *video* customers—and never had a chance in the music business.

Huizenga's buying spree continued with the purchase of production companies Republic Pictures and Spelling Entertainment, a kids' indoor playland called Discovery Zone, an adult gaming complex called Block Party, and amphitheaters for concerts. He even bought land in Florida to build a theme park to compete with Disney World. Blockbuster had been so successful that many, including much of Wall Street, believed this expansion of the Blockbuster brand made perfect sense, and its stock continued to rise even as store sales growth began to slow. But in a few years, every one of the businesses Blockbuster bought to expand the brand failed. And, of course, "BlockbusterLand" never got built.

Blockbuster's history could have been very different, had it used this time and flood of cash to commit more resources to improve the business instead of having a singular focus on growth. In its race to open stores faster than anyone else, Blockbuster made hundreds of real estate mistakes, accepting inferior locations in its haste to open 3,000 stores in six years. These poorly located stores were underperforming, but more importantly, were extremely vulnerable to the inevitable competition to come. Blockbuster occasionally relocated stores to correct these situations, but they desperately needed a more comprehensive approach to the problem. Several cities were littered with inferior sites that had no chance of survival in more difficult times. Other markets had been overbuilt to block competitors.

And while Blockbuster sat on the largest movie database in the world and did very little with it, others were already using their own information to develop a superior consumer proposition. Blockbuster did not recognize it at the time, but they had *not* created a great company that was built to last. Its stores were essentially the same as the first that opened in 1985. What they *had* done is build a very big company and made thousands of people rich beyond their wildest dreams. But they did it by being first—not by being best.

Huizenga feared others would copy Blockbuster, which is why he grew the company at such startling speed. But he never seemed to consider that others could do it *better*, that stores opened across the street from a Blockbuster store could slash its profit by 75 percent. But that was already happening in the early 1990s. Perhaps they were too small to get Blockbuster's attention, but competitors had already decimated dozens of Blockbuster stores by giving customers more of what they wanted—much more than

Blockbuster. The biggest and most successful ones were being run by a "little old grocery store company from Texas" called H-E-B.

CHAPTER 3

THAT LITTLE OLD GROCERY STORE COMPANY FROM TEXAS

"H-E-B Chairman Charles Butt is still the greatest living leader, student, and teacher of retail."

—BURT FLICKINGER, MANAGING DIRECTOR,
STRATEGIC RESOURCE GROUP

This book is the story of Blockbuster. What does H-E-B, a grocery company many have never heard of, have to do with it? Answer: in 1992, it was the largest remaining direct competitor of Blockbuster. But this is not a story about H-E-B grocery stores, although they did rent videos in small departments like most grocery companies of the day. No, this is a story about a freestanding video store that H-E-B created called Video Central. There were only 35 of them, but almost all competed directly with Blockbuster and dominated them in head-to-head competition. Sales at Blockbuster stores that competed with Video Central were about half its national average, and the Video Central stores across the street were profitably generating sales two to three times that of Blockbuster.

In the entire history of the video business, Video Central was the *only* chain of video stores created by an established retail company, not by entrepreneurs who were often undercapitalized and jumped at the first opportunity to profitably exit the business. And, in this case, that retail company was H-E-B, widely regarded as the best grocery company in the U.S., as well as one of the best retailers of any kind.

H-E-B is also the company I worked with for 15 years, the last seven running store operations for the Video Central chain. It is where I learned retailing first and the video business second. After leaving H-E-B in 1993, I spent 25 years as a Blockbuster franchisee, yet learned virtually nothing from them about how to manage a sustainable business. I succeeded despite Blockbuster's race to failure because of the business principles I learned while at H-E-B.

Even though Blockbuster was the flagship brand of the industry in 1993, Video Central's dominance of them in places like San Antonio and Austin illustrated how vulnerable they had become. But with only 35 stores, Video Central was tiny when compared to Blockbuster's 3,000. Perhaps that is why Blockbuster never took them seriously and often referred to them as the stores run by that "little old grocery store company from Texas." But what would happen if somebody copied what Video Central was doing and opened a couple of thousand stores? Unfortunately for Block-buster, that is exactly what happened.

Who is H-E-B? If you have ever lived in Central or South Texas or Houston, you already know about them. If you have moved away from one of those areas, you miss it greatly because you now understand that nobody does it like H-E-B. In Central and South Texas, home to two of the fastest-growing cities in America, Austin and San Antonio, H-E-B's market share is over 60 percent—unheard of in the grocery business. In 2020, the company operates over 330 stores in Texas and Mexico that generate over $26 billion in annual sales. Their average annual store sales of over $80 million are the highest of any grocery chain in the country. In H-E-B territory, about the only reason to shop a competitor is if you don't like crowds. You can find plenty of peace and quiet there.

H-E-B is one of the largest privately-owned companies in the U.S. Its Chairman, Charles Butt, has run the company since he took over for his father in 1971 (the initials H.E.B. are for his father, Howard Edward Butt). He does not speak a lot publicly, and when he does, he normally attributes H-E-B's success to others. But as illustrated by the quote at the beginning of this chapter, he is regarded by many as one of the great business leaders in the world.

H-E-B has been named the best grocery company in the country by many, and most recently by the 2020 Dunnhumby Retailer Preference Index, ahead of Trader Joe's, Whole Foods, Costco, Walmart, Publix, and everyone else. The 2019 Glassdoor survey of the Top 100 CEOs in the country ranks Charles Butt number 2 with a 99 percent approval rating among employees. The Temkin Group's annual survey that measures customers' trust in companies ranks H-E-B near the top every year, and in 2017, ranked them number 1—just ahead of Mercedes-Benz. In 2019,

Indeed.com, the nation's number 1 job site, ranked H-E-B as the best retailer in the country to work for. Awards like this have been showered on H-E-B for years. It is a special company but, remarkably, Blockbuster never took them seriously.

As I write this book, the country is learning how fragile the supply chain is for the grocery industry. The spread of the coronavirus has caused mass shortages of virtually every product in stores. Manufacturers cannot ship to warehouses fast enough. Trucks cannot deliver to stores fast enough. And the stores are not sufficiently designed or staffed to keep shelves full. Even the best companies do not have the infrastructure to keep pace with demand. But as has always been the case, H-E-B successfully met the challenge, so much so that a Texas state legislator proclaimed, "H-E-B for president!"

Although the coronavirus pandemic is a rare and hopefully one-time event, it illustrates the complexity of the grocery business. And it is extremely competitive with razor-thin profit margins. Small errors and inefficiencies can lead to staggering losses, but small incremental improvements can lead to extraordinary gains. The best grocery companies successfully manage a myriad of details and make small improvements every year. Those who do not eventually fail.

Grocery stores are really several stores in one, especially the large, high-volume ones like H-E-B. All the various departments have unique challenges. The fresh produce department, for example, is managed quite differently from the dry grocery department and all the others like frozen foods, dairy, drugs, floral, etc. Successful companies develop hundreds of diagnostic tools to evaluate performance that are managed by a staff of hundreds in every store. It is impossible to measure everything, but great companies like H-E-B have figured out what matters, and they relentlessly track and pursue perfection in those areas. Although the video store business had its own unique challenges, it was never as complex, competitive, or unforgiving as the grocery business. It was a relatively simple business for a company like H-E-B to manage, and they did it very, very well.

When Video Central opened its first store in 1987, H-E-B was not as large or well-known as today, but they were not a secret in retail circles. One keen observer was Sam Walton. The Walmart stores in those days were primarily general merchandise stores. They carried a selection of nonperishable staples, but unlike today, they were not a primary destination for grocery shoppers. But Walton knew they needed to be and, to jump-start this new business, he hired an H-E-B manager to launch Walmart's new food business. These early stores were called Hypermarts, and they were run by Rich Donckers, a regional manager for H-E-B for seven years and personally hired by Walton. Donckers brought several other H-E-B managers with him. Today, Walmart is by far the largest seller of food in the country and, of course, the largest brick-and-mortar retailer in the world.

As successful as H-E-B has become, they remain obsessed with being not just first or biggest but also best. Today, they are at the forefront of developing home delivery, curbside pickup, and many other initiatives to meet the ever-changing preferences of food shoppers. Although H-E-B has become a Texas institution, it is never self-congratulatory. They are never satisfied with where they are because tomorrow they *must* be better.

This is the environment in which I learned retailing. Competitive. Never satisfied. Constantly searching for ways to improve. It is why every new H-E-B store that opens is a little different from the last. Charles Butt knows that companies that do not improve every year could be gone the next. It is a way of life at H-E-B and always has been. I spent fifteen years in that environment, and it is why I never understood the Blockbuster way of "build, baby, build" with almost no consideration for how the business could be *managed better*.

How did Video Central so successfully compete with Blockbuster, and why couldn't others do the same? Because it was the perfect marriage of a successful retail organization and one of the best entrepreneurial minds in the video rental business, Craig Odanovich. He was one of those early retailers who began renting videos when he learned customers wouldn't pay $100 to buy them. He owned a large, successful music store in Corpus Christi, Texas, called Craig's Record Factory. Craig understood how inventory management and competitive pricing drove volume and captured market share. Although large chains like Sound Warehouse and Tower Records dominated the music business in those days, none had stores in Corpus Christi because Craig's Record Factory already dominated the market.

When he started renting videos, he applied the same market-share-driven strategy and was one of the earliest to recognize the huge potential of this new business. Craig began exploring expansion options, but instead of opening freestanding video stores, he chose to partner with H-E-B to take immediate advantage of all the foot traffic their stores generated every day. In 1981, he and Roger Davidson, an H-E-B general merchandise manager, tested small video rental departments in a few H-E-B stores, and it was a runaway success. Soon, Craig had 60 departments with plans to open more and upgrade others to a larger "store-in-store" concept meant to compete with the larger video stores of the day (Blockbuster, for example).

The success of the early video departments got H-E-B's attention. Video rental was becoming a reason to go to the grocery store. Soon, grocery stores across the country would capture 25 percent of the entire video rental market, and H-E-B knew it needed to be in the business in a big way. As was typical of H-E-B, if they were going to be in a business, they wanted to dominate it; and they believed that could best be achieved by owning the business instead of continuing to partner with Craig. So, in 1986, they struck a deal with Craig to buy his business. Craig and his entire support team joined H-E-B to continue growing what had become a nationwide phenomenon. Renting movies was going mainstream, and H-E-B wanted to be a part of it. But they weren't content with only video departments in their grocery stores.

In 1987, just a few months after H-E-B had bought Craig's company, Blockbuster already had three stores open in San Antonio and was looking for more sites. That led them to H-E-B, which owned several shopping centers around town. But instead of leasing to Blockbuster, someone at H-E-B asked the question: "If this is such a great business, why don't we do it ourselves? Let's get Craig to do it! And let's not just do one. Let's build a chain of them in towns with H-E-B grocery stores."

That chain would be called Video Central, and the management team was assembled. Craig would head it up. I had run H-E-B grocery stores for the past seven years and was asked to lead store operations. Roger Davidson, who had championed the first video departments in grocery stores, would head up marketing. Greg Smith, a lifetime friend of Craig and a successful entrepreneur himself, joined to lead technology and inventory management. In addition, we had the support and guidance of H-E-B's entire executive team.

The first Video Central store opened in San Antonio in 1987 and, like the first Blockbuster, was an immediate success, surpassing all our sales goals. A few weeks later, a new Blockbuster store opened across the street, and that is when we knew we were on to something. Nothing happened! Sales hardly moved. We counted Blockbuster's customers, and estimated their new store was doing less than half the sales of the new Video Central. Block-buster had attracted customers but had taken few, if any, of ours. Then we launched a decidedly low-tech way to confirm our esti-mate of the Blockbuster store's sales. We grabbed trash from their dumpster and found sales reports that caused a small celebration around the office. The shiny new Blockbuster store was doing about $8,000 a week in sales. The Video Central across the street: $25,000!

Any doubt that H-E-B and Video Central could compete with Blockbuster was now erased, and we went into expansion mode. Over the next few years, we opened another 34 stores. Not all of them competed directly with Blockbuster, but those that did routinely doubled its sales and, in some cases, like the first store, tripled it.

Craig brought a business model to H-E-B and Video Central that was like *kryptonite* to Blockbuster. Prices were lower, and inventories were larger and much better managed. We ran it just like H-E-B ran grocery stores. Define what matters most and relentlessly pursue perfection in those areas. And do your best to make it fun for employees and customers. That was not all that hard to do in a video store, which was a fun place to work and an equally fun place for customers.

As those first stores opened, one thing continued to confuse us. We were decimating every Blockbuster with which we competed, but they never responded. They never adjusted the price and continued to be out of important new releases every weekend. Blockbuster did not seem to care. We did notice they increased advertising, especially television. But it was the same generic national message they were running everywhere else and had no impact.

Even though Blockbuster never made substantive changes to compete with Video Central, we always feared they would. And just like H-E-B, we were never satisfied and continued to search for ways to gain even the slightest advantage. This led to a game-changing strategy that transformed much of the video rental industry.

In those early years, all movies at Video Central, as well as most other video stores, rented for one day at a time. But Blockbuster rented them for two days, although they confusingly called it "three evenings" because they were due back by 7 p.m. on the third day. We always considered our one-day rental at Video Central stores a potential weakness. All movies rented Friday were due back Saturday, which could be inconvenient for some customers.

It was Greg Smith who first asked the question: "We only need the high-demand new releases back the next day. Why don't we extend the rental period for everything else?" To which many of us answered: "Wouldn't that confuse customers because some movies would be due back the next day and some not?" But like so many other ideas we tested at Video Central, the answer to that question was: "Let the customer decide. Let them vote with their dollars."

Greg's challenge led to the development of the five-day rental period. Why five and not more, maybe a week? It was simple. About 70 percent of all rentals occurred on the weekend. A movie rented Saturday would be back Thursday and available for the next weekend. If the rental period was more than five days, the movie would be out for two weekends, which *doubled* the demand on each store's inventory. We went to a 5-day rental period for every movie in the store except new releases and, as a bonus, did not raise the price for the extra days.

We rolled out the plan, and customers loved it! Very few had problems returning new releases the next day and understood why. The 5-day rental period, which applied to about 95 percent of the inventory, was a huge hit. Customers rented more movies; many rented a half dozen or more to keep for several days. It was the early days of what was later called "binge-watching." Those six movies cost $6 to rent for five days at Video Central. The same movies were rented for $18 and two days at Blockbuster. We stole even more of their customers, yet they *never* responded.

The Video Central approach to the business was all about value and abundance, which was a concept a long line of Blockbuster

CEOs would never understand. Video Central stores rented about *three times more movies* than the typical Blockbuster store, and inventory management became a critical component of everything we did. Greg Smith built a system I would later learn was far superior to anything at Blockbuster. He did it with the support of H-E-B's MIS department, which had also written the code for the store computer system. He even designed and built a warehouse and distribution system to store and move product from store to store to maximize in-stock conditions. This created another distinct advantage Blockbuster never matched.

Roger Davidson built an aggressive marketing campaign that screamed our fun, low-price approach to the business. He worked with H-E-B's advertising department to customize the message and media buys, as well as set up important sponsorships. For example, Video Central was a major sponsor of the San Antonio Spurs and featured Gregg Popovich (an assistant coach then) and Spurs legend Sean Elliot on a movie review show.

Video Central stores were early *laboratories* of the business. Because we had access to H-E-B's distribution system, we tested hundreds of products and fine-tuned the inventory to what customers wanted. Early on, we learned that video store customers wanted two things: movies and snacks. That was all. There were a handful of exceptions over the years, but they were insignificant to store economics. In the coming years, Blockbuster would waste hundreds of millions testing the same products we did in those early years—with the same results. Customers wanted movies and snacks, the same as when they went to a movie theater. It is where all the focus should have been. But right up to its bankruptcy, Blockbuster was still trying to *sell* things customers would not buy in video rental stores.

In addition to the Video Central stores, the departments inside H-E-B grocery stores continued to grow. The "store-in-store" concept was rolled out and called Video Central Express. Although these self-contained stores were about one-fourth the size of a Blockbuster, they generated comparable sales.

With over a hundred locations combined, Video Central stores and the departments inside H-E-B stores dominated the video rental market in central and south Texas from 1987 to 1993. Although small by Blockbuster standards, it was a fully developed video rental machine that was superior in every way and backed by one of the country's best retail organizations. Yet, Blockbuster never seemed to care or notice and never did anything differently to answer our challenge; they just opened more stores.

In 1992, Video Central was named Retailer of the Year by the Video Software Dealers Association (VSDA), of which Craig was a four-term member of its Board of Directors (Wayne Huizenga was also a member). Video Central won the award over Target stores, one of the other finalists. We had hit our stride and had even ventured outside H-E-B markets by opening four stores in the Houston area. (H-E-B is the market leader in Houston now but did not have stores there in 1992.) The Houston stores were successful, but we began to focus our expansion plans on the franchise-owned markets that Blockbuster had been slow to develop. The opportunities were greater there. Arizona was the most promising, and Craig had begun to broach the subject with H-E-B when the rug was pulled out from under us.

Charles Butt decided he did not want to open any more Video Central stores outside H-E-B markets, even Houston. That decision would severely limit our growth potential because we had built out most H-E-B markets by this time. And it would restrict the management team's professional growth as well. So he began to explore opportunities to sell the Video Central stores in hopes that the team could move on and continue their careers in the business we had all come to love—maybe even with Blockbuster.

It came as no surprise that Huizenga had an interest in buying Video Central, and two H-E-B officers were dispatched to Blockbuster's Ft. Lauderdale headquarters to meet with him and Steve Berrard in late 1992. But surprisingly, the negotiations went nowhere. The H-E-B representatives made it clear the deal would be contingent on Blockbuster finding comparable roles for the Video Central management team. That did not seem to appeal to him, and the discussions ended. Huizenga and Berrard never even looked at the financial information; if they had, it might have changed their minds.

It is impossible to know precisely why Huizenga wasn't more interested in buying Video Central. He was knee-deep in much larger acquisitions, like the music stores and the land in Florida for BlockbusterLand and, personally, with his professional sports teams. And he was already having preliminary discussions about selling Blockbuster to Viacom, which would happen less than two years later. Or perhaps it was because he always had more control of the negotiations when he bought video stores. The small video companies Huizenga typically bought were usually looking for a profitable exit before Blockbuster opened stores to compete with them. Huizenga almost always held the upper hand. But H-E-B was a bigger company than Blockbuster and, because of its success against them, had no reason to fear them. This was a relatively small transaction for H-E-B too, and they were in no hurry to sell.

The important point is, had Blockbuster paid more attention to its competition, they would have known to pursue this transaction. Video Central's average store sales were higher than Blockbuster's, and they were much more profitable. Plus, sales at all the Blockbuster stores that competed with Video Central were far below its national average (we knew this from all our trash runs). They should have wanted to know why.

In addition, the video departments inside H-E-B supermarkets were very successful, with many generating comparable sales to Blockbuster stores. Nationally, grocery stores were already generating over $1 billion in video rental sales, and that would soon grow to over $2 billion—25 percent of the entire market. Blockbuster needed to better understand that part of the business, and they could have by hiring the people who ran it at H-E-B like Sam Walton did when he hired H-E-B people to teach Walmart the grocery business.

But in retrospect, it is not surprising that Huizenga had so little interest in H-E-B and Video Central. Neither he nor the entire Blockbuster organization ever showed much interest in its competitors except to buy them. And in this case, the decision not to buy Video Central would prove to be one of their biggest mistakes. Why? Because it soon gave rise to the largest brick-and-mortar competitor Blockbuster ever had—and its first financial crisis.

We had heard about a small chain of video stores in Oregon

called Hollywood Video that was using a business model much like Video Central's. And we soon learned that its owner, Mark Wattles, had befriended our movie buyer, who had been sharing way too much information about how we did things. Wattles had learned how our business model worked and that it was extremely effective against Blockbuster. Our buyer had been all too eager to tell the story and, after copying much of it, Wattles' stores were getting the same results.

Wattles was an astute businessperson and had big plans. He had patterned his stores after Video Central, and buying them would be the perfect opportunity to jump-start growth. He began negotiating with H-E-B about buying the Video Central stores and soon agreed to a deal. The most difficult part of the transaction was negotiating the transition plan for the Video Central management team, an issue that appeared to have stalled talks with Blockbuster. But Wattles accommodated H-E-B and closed the deal.

In July 1993, with the purchase agreement to buy Video Central in hand, Wattles raised $12 million with an initial public stock offering, larger than the one that provided the initial capital to start Blockbuster. Two months later, he closed the deal to buy 33 of the 35 Video Central stores for $30.5 million—his first acquisition. (Two stores that were adjoined to H-E-B grocery stores were not included in the sale.) The average price paid per store was $942,000, which must have shocked Blockbuster because, as I would later learn, they thought the stores were barely profitable.

Most of the Video Central management team joined Hollywood Video—all the store managers and much of the support staff, including regional managers and our controller. It was not just a transfer of store ownership but a transfer of knowledge built competing with Blockbuster over the last seven years. Craig Odanovich joined them as Chief Operations Officer and moved to Portland, OR. I left to join a Blockbuster franchise group, which is discussed in the next chapter. Roger Davidson had already been assigned to a different project and has since held several executive positions at H-E-B and other grocery companies. Greg Smith moved back to his hometown of Flour Bluff, just outside of Corpus Christi, where he owns businesses and is a member of the city council.

Hollywood Video had just 15 stores when it bought Video Central in 1993. Just three years later, they were operating 550! They opened their 1,000th store in early 1998 and had almost 2,000 by the turn of the century. Their strategy for growth was much like that of Video Central. Find the highest-volume Blockbuster stores and open across the street. It was a simple plan and extremely effective. Most importantly, it demonstrated the vulnerability of Blockbuster's business model. They were not invincible—far from it.

After buying Video Central, Hollywood Video quickly became Blockbuster's *only national competitor.* Would that be the case had they not bought Video Central in 1993? Perhaps, but certainly not as quickly. As the largest and most successful competitor of Blockbuster, Video Central provided the store base and strong cash flow Wattles needed to ramp up the company's pace of growth. Had Blockbuster bought the stores, the scenario would have been much different.

This story was ignored by Wall Street and led analysts to erroneous conclusions about what went wrong with Blockbuster a few years later. When Blockbuster's financials began to weaken, it was blamed on everything *but* Hollywood Video by most. But Tom Adams, a longtime media industry analyst, got it right when he wrote:

> "Blockbuster has stronger competition now than they ever had before from Hollywood Video and some of the other chains that have recently beefed up their presence. But frankly, the only one of all the chains that are building stores of the size and punch in the market as Blockbuster is Hollywood."[17]

As Hollywood Video ramped up its store openings, Blockbuster sales growth immediately slowed, and its cash flow even more so. Hollywood was targeting Blockbuster's highest volume, most profitable stores, just as we had done at Video Central. For this reason, the damage Hollywood Video was inflicting on Blockbuster's bottom line was disproportionate to the number of stores it opened.

Video rental was a largely fixed-cost business, which means as sales declined, much of the cost to run the store stays the same. For most video stores, including Blockbuster, every $1.00 lost in sales resulted in a minimum $.50 loss to cash flow. When Hollywood Video opened across the street from a Blockbuster store that was generating $1 million in sales and $300,000 in cash flow, sales typically declined about 40 percent, or $400,000. But cash flow would decline by about 66 percent, or $200,000. This happened hundreds of times in the years immediately after Hollywood Video bought Video Central.

Blockbuster's annual cash flow at the time was about $700

million. Five hundred Hollywood stores could therefore cut Blockbuster's cash flow by $100 million. One thousand stores by $200 million. And so on. The results were devastating, yet Blockbuster had no answers and did nothing about it—except spend millions opening more stores, even as Hollywood was picking off their best ones. In 1997, just four years after Hollywood Video bought Video Central, Blockbuster was cash flow negative and on the verge of total collapse.

Blockbuster management would change during that period, but no one acknowledged what Hollywood Video had done to them, nor did they do anything about it. In fact, they made it worse by continuing to run stores the same as the first that opened in 1985. More and more, Blockbuster was out of touch with the market, long before advances in digital technology became a factor. Prices were too high, inventories too small, and the availability of new releases worse than ever.

Craig Odanovich and the Video Central management team did not fully understand it in 1993, but we had created a business model that was years ahead of its time. We understood that keeping new releases in stock was always the number one goal of a video store and the best way to do so was by renting them one day at a time, which maximized the number of rents and satisfied the most customers. Led by Greg Smith, we also built analytical tools to forecast demand for each title. As our database grew, so did the accuracy of new release purchases. *Twenty years later*, Redbox effectively used the same one-day new release strategy pioneered by Video Central to effectively finish off Blockbuster. Today, it is the largest video rental company still standing.

Craig also understood that older movies were a crucial part of the video store experience, but customers expected to pay less for them than new releases, the same as for older movies in theaters. Video Central stores' catalog inventories were more than twice the size of the typical Blockbuster and rented for $1, one-third of Blockbuster's standard price of $3 at the time. But even though they were priced less, they rented so often that Video Central's catalog movies generated much more sales than a typical Blockbuster. More importantly, Video Central customers became movie buffs and had more reasons to come to the stores than to just rent the new release of the week. They rented *more* catalog movies than new releases, a concept Blockbuster never understood. Years later, Netflix by-mail used a similar approach by building an intensely loyal customer base renting primarily older movies. That sent Blockbuster into a decline from which it never recovered.

Perhaps most startling, Blockbuster never even tested either of these strategies, choosing instead to do the exact opposite. Over the years, they continued to raise the price for new releases, which helped give rise to Redbox's low-price approach. And even as Netflix was demonstrating how consumer tastes were *expanding*, Blockbuster's selection of catalog titles was *shrinking*.

Blockbuster made a lot of mistakes, as all companies do. But its biggest came from its lack of curiosity about competitors. Blockbuster could have learned a lot from them but was *never* interested until it was too late. In the case of Video Central, Blockbuster paid a huge price for ignoring Craig Odanovich's business model. It contained important concepts they needed to understand, concepts that in a few years would be used by Netflix and Redbox to destroy the company.

CHAPTER 4

WELCOME TO BLOCKBUSTER

"Success is a lousy teacher. It seduces smart people into thinking they can't lose."

—BILL GATES, CO-FOUNDER OF MICROSOFT

By 1993, almost all of Blockbuster's sales growth was coming from new stores. Sales at many of its existing ones had hit a wall, and some were already in decline. For six straight years, Blockbuster had caught the new video rental industry flatfooted as it opened hundreds of stores every year. But even though millions more Americans were renting movies each year, cracks were beginning to show in Blockbuster's singular strategy of "build, baby, build." Retired President Luigi Salvaneschi had seen it coming. "Customers are suffering, and you need to put more emphasis on the stores." He could have added: "If you don't do it, competitors will."

Video Central was one of several smaller companies that found Blockbuster easy prey. Hundreds of Blockbuster stores, corporately owned and franchise alike, had already been negatively impacted by smaller companies that seemed to better understand the business. One of these struggling Blockbuster franchisees was owned by a cable television company based in Austin, Texas, called Prime Cable. They had bought the rights to develop the state of Alaska in 1989 and opened eight stores. The early years went so well they followed that by buying the franchise rights to El Paso, Texas, where they opened ten more. Prime had followed the Blockbuster playbook, but recently, locally-owned competitors in Alaska had learned how to steal their customers. Sales growth had stalled, and they were even considering closing some of their Alaskan stores because they were losing money. No new stores were planned.

Prime Cable was founded by cable television legend Bob Hughes, who had been in the business since its early days in the 1960s. It was a highly respected company in the industry, and Hughes, along with two other Prime executives, was later elected to the Cable Television Hall of Fame. Prime owned the cable system in Anchorage, Alaska, as well as larger ones in Atlanta, Chicago, Las Vegas, and other cities. It was one of three cable television companies that owned Blockbuster franchise stores. United Cable was the second-largest franchise group in the system with 112 stores, and Cox Cable owned 82 stores. All three had been recruited by Blockbuster to help counter the persistent Wall Street belief that cable television's pay-per-view offerings would make video stores obsolete. Why would a cable television company invest in Blockbuster if that were true?

United and Cox were not in the business for long. They sold their stores back to Blockbuster in 1993 and 1989, respectively. But

Prime did not have that luxury. Blockbuster had no interest in operating stores in remote Alaska, especially since the stores were beginning to struggle.

Managing retail stores bore no resemblance to running a cable television system. As successful as Prime Cable had been, these cable television veterans had no answers when competitors began to steal their Blockbuster customers. And they only made matters worse when they raised prices and tried to promote their way out of the problem, believing the Blockbuster brand would eventually win out. Prime had made many of the same mistakes Blockbuster would repeatedly make in coming years. But unlike Blockbuster, Prime was open to listening to another point of view, especially to someone from H-E-B, a company with which they were familiar. In early 1993, they called me to talk about managing their stores, and since H-E-B had made it known Video Central was for sale, I jumped at the opportunity to talk.

In my early conversations with Prime, I learned franchisees had total control over price, rental terms, and how late fees were administered. As to inventory, there were general guidelines, but franchisees essentially called their own shots. And as was often misunderstood, Blockbuster did not provide movies to franchisees. Those were purchased from distribution companies on terms separately negotiated with the studios. Franchisees were required to use the Blockbuster store computer system and support the brand by adhering to certain usage guidelines. But beyond that, they ran their businesses as they saw fit. I saw opportunity.

Hollywood Video had already begun talking to H-E-B about

buying the Video Central stores, so as much as I had enjoyed my 15 years there, I decided to leave in April 1993 to become President of Prime Video and lead their 18 stores. And as had so many done when they joined Blockbuster, I took a pay cut in exchange for a small amount of ownership in hopes I could grow the company over the next few years.

For the past seven years, my total focus had been on how to *beat* Blockbuster, but now I was joining their team. I planned to combine Video Central's proven business model with the dominant Blockbuster brand. The plan worked perfectly, and soon, we were one of the largest and most successful franchise groups in the company.

But unlike the Prime Cable owners, Blockbuster never showed interest in other points of view. In the coming years, there would be *five* different Blockbuster management teams, but none were interested in how we ran our business. The common theme was always, "Not invented here? Not interested." Call it arrogance, hubris, denial—whatever. But for the entire life of the company, Blockbuster management never had the ability to consider views other than its own.

My first experience at Blockbuster set the tone for the next 25 years. I attended a national franchise meeting in Ft. Lauderdale in the spring of 1993. I watched with a degree of awe as Wayne Huizenga transfixed the gathering with his thoughts about Blockbuster's accomplishments and what the future held. Most in the audience had unquestioned loyalty for Huizenga and rightly so. They had made fortunes following him.

But what struck me most was the complete lack of discussion

about the stores, other than to open more. There was no discussion about how Blockbuster needed to answer the growing number of successful competitors. In two days of meetings, they were never even mentioned. Although many like Video Central had been successfully competing with Blockbuster, it seemed that they were all too small to warrant Blockbuster's attention. The theme of the meeting was completely self-congratulatory. It focused only on how great Blockbuster was. Not much was said about how to make it better—just bigger. The overriding theme of the meeting was "Open more stores. Make lots of money. Repeat."

The fact that Video Central was for sale only added to their belief that competitors did not warrant their attention. I tried to talk to several corporate executives about Video Central in hopes we could share some ideas. But their response was clear. "We won. You lost. Get over it." From their perspective, there was nothing to talk about.

The grocery industry in which H-E-B thrived is well-known as a low margin business. Successful companies take only three or four cents of every dollar of sales to the bottom line. But those pennies on the dollar generate a healthy return on investment, which is the ultimate measure of any successful business. Blockbuster had convinced themselves that because Video Central was owned by a grocery company, its profit margins were the same: three or four cents on the dollar. But the video rental business model was much different from grocery stores. It required higher profit margins to generate an acceptable return on investment, but evidently, Blockbuster did not think H-E-B was smart enough to figure that out—remarkable, given its long track record of success.

I knew, of course, that Video Central's profit margin was comparable to Blockbuster's. When I tried to explain this to a Blockbuster executive, he told me that I did not know what I was talking about. For seven years, I had complete responsibility for managing the financial performance of Video Central stores, yet *he* knew better. It was a revealing exchange. At Blockbuster, denial was always easier than searching for the truth.

Undeterred, I remained persistent in my attempts to "talk shop" with Blockbuster management. A few weeks after the national franchise meeting, the Vice President of Franchising, Bob Guerin, visited our El Paso stores. Guerin was an official member of the "Friends of Wayne" club, so his visit was a special occasion. He had been a Vice President for Huizenga at Waste Management but before that was President of Wells Fargo Armored Service Corporation—the company that moved all the money around in those armored cars. Like all "Friends of Wayne," he had no experience in retail prior to Blockbuster.

I had hoped the store visits would be more businesslike than the celebratory atmosphere of the national franchise meeting. Perhaps we could talk in more detail about how Blockbuster stores operated and ways we could all improve. But the store visits did not provide the right opportunity to broach the subject. The visits were quick, superficial, and only focused on "following the rules." Perhaps dinner would be a better opportunity to talk details about the business, so that evening, I suggested to Guerin there were some things about Video Central that Blockbuster should know. Their business model dominated Blockbuster in head-to-head competition, and now, Hollywood Video would be deploying it on a much larger scale. Let's discuss. Guerin looked at me with a condescending scowl I can still see and feel today. He had been waiting all day to put me in my place. "You're with Blockbuster now," he barked. "You need to get over that!" He quickly changed the subject, and it was never discussed again.

Guerin was known to be tough and often rude, and I had gotten a full dose of it, but nothing close to what Fred Montesi experienced. Fred was one of the first Blockbuster franchisees and one of the largest. He owned stores in Nashville, Memphis, and other towns in central and western Tennessee, plus managed more for other franchisees. For the entire history of Blockbuster, he was one of the largest and most successful franchisees. But that did not exempt him from Guerin's tactics. In a meeting with Guerin about some contentious development questions, Fred was shocked when Guerin pulled a handgun from his trousers and calmly placed it on the table. Fred never believed Guerin intended to use it other than as a tool of intimidation, and that message had been clearly delivered. It was vintage Bob Guerin.

Guerin used a different intimidation tactic on me. After the El Paso store visits, he had the director of franchising call a superior at Prime Cable to inform him I was a "spy" for Hollywood Video. But it was just the opposite. I was trying to *warn* Blockbuster about what was to come. For seven years, I ran the same business model at Video Central and knew things about Hollywood Video that Blockbuster needed to understand. But neither Guerin nor anyone else at Blockbuster was interested.

So, just a few weeks into my 25-year career as a Blockbuster franchisee, the rules of engagement had been clearly defined. Follow the rules, keep your mouth shut, and everything will be just fine. I got the message loud and clear.

Fortunately for me and everyone at Prime, Blockbuster could intimidate and shut down discussion, but they couldn't tell us how to run our stores. With access to all their numbers, I started digging into the guts of how Blockbuster did things. I had battled them for seven years. Now I was able to really understand what made them tick and decide how we were going to run our Blockbuster stores in Alaska and El Paso.

This part of the story gets a little technical, but it is important to understanding the mindset of Blockbuster and why the company was already starting to decline in 1993. Video rental was always about how to manage the two primary parts of the business, *new releases* and *catalog,* and the two were totally different. Managing new releases was always about staying in stock as best you could with movies that cost $65 and had to be rented 22 times just to break even. These movies hit the stores every Tuesday, and the peak demand lasted only about two weeks. It was a race to rent them as many times as possible before demand began to decline.

The management of older movies, the catalog, was different. How many titles should a store stock, and how should they be priced? By now, the studios had dug into their vaults and released about every title that mattered, at least 15,000 of them. Demand for these titles varied drastically among stores, so there were a lot of decisions to make.

The Video Central approach to the business was like night and day to Blockbuster's. Given our success against them while at H-E-B,

I always wondered why they never changed. Our availability of new releases was far better than theirs, and it was obvious from visiting their stores that customers did not pay much attention to their catalog movies. Perhaps there was something under the hood I did not understand, and now as a Blockbuster franchisee, I was about to find out.

The video store business was all about weekends. About 70 percent of all the week's business occurred Fridays and Saturdays. Stores would typically rent every copy of high-demand new releases on Fridays. Video Central rented new releases one day at a time. Rent it Friday. Return it Saturday so it could be rented again. Blockbuster rented them for two days. Rent it Friday. Return it *Sunday*. At Video Central, movies were back on the shelf Saturday to be rented again. At Blockbuster, they were not returned until Sunday, which meant their stores were out of stock on most new release titles on busy Saturday nights. It was as simple as that.

Video Central stores had more new releases in stock, which meant more happy customers. Plus, Video Central generated *two* rents per copy on Friday and Saturday nights, Blockbuster, only *one*. The Video Central approach not only satisfied more customers, but it also generated more rents and more sales, which allowed it to buy more copies and satisfy even more customers. It was not unusual for a Video Central store to have four times more copies of a hot new release title than Blockbuster.

The Video Central approach was inherently more efficient. That was undeniable. More rents. More sales. More copies. The only question was the perceived value of Blockbuster's 2-day rental term. Did customers place more value on how long they could keep a movie than whether or not it was available to rent? In central and south Texas, that question had already been answered. More than twice as many customers came to Video Central stores than Blockbuster stores. Would they do the same in our Blockbuster stores in Alaska and El Paso? We were about to find out.

Then there was the question of catalog movies. Again, Blockbuster managed this massive selection of movies completely differently than Video Central. About 15,000 titles were available from studios; Video Central stocked about 50 percent more of them than Blockbuster and rented them for $1. Blockbuster's smaller inventory rented for $3, the same as new releases. It had never made sense to us that Blockbuster charged the same price for old movies as new ones. Customers never saw it that way either. Otherwise, there would have been no discount theaters showing older movies at prices that were a fraction of those for first-run movies.

But was Blockbuster using its massive database to so effectively match titles to customer demand that it could charge a higher price? Finding the answer to that question was difficult, almost impossible. Their systems for managing catalog titles were elementary. And I was astounded to learn that there was not a report in the Blockbuster computer system that broke out the rentals of the catalog sections of its stores.

Let me say that again. Blockbuster did not even *know* how many rentals came from their catalog sections—the Drama, Comedy, Action, and Horror categories you saw on your way to the new release wall. If you asked that question of ten different Blockbuster executives, you would get ten different answers. I did just that in a meeting with top Blockbuster executives a few years later, and still, they did not know and did not care. These movies occupied at least 50 percent of the sales floor in Blockbuster stores, but the company never had an effective way to track them. At Prime, we built workaround systems to track them and knew exactly how they rented in our stores. Blockbuster never did.

After two months of studying the Blockbuster way, we knew what to do. We turned our stores upside down. We increased the inventory of new releases and began renting them a day at a time. Then we cut the price of titles in the catalog section in half and began strategically adding to the inventory as rentals increased.

The immediacy and degree of the turnaround were shocking, and we had not even advertised it. Sales immediately increased by 20 percent, even more in some stores. The store in Wasilla, Alaska, increased over 40 percent and won the President's Award that year for being the highest-growth store in the entire franchise system.

And the catalog movies? Rentals skyrocketed as much as 500 percent! Customers really *did* care about price. Even though we had dropped the price of the catalog by over 60 percent, sales went up. Customers were coming in droves and roaming the entire store, not just the new release wall. Our entire company was energized. Instead of closing stores, we opened twelve more in the next few years. We would continue to tweak and improve, but the foundation had been laid. Sales and profits continued to grow for the next fifteen years, long after Blockbuster was on the brink of failure.

Given the drastic improvement of our Alaska and El Paso stores, one would think Blockbuster would have had at least a passing interest in what caused it. But by this time, I knew better. There were no questions and no discussions—zero interest in what we did to produce such drastic improvement, the most dramatic in the entire Blockbuster system.

Representatives from the Blockbuster franchise department would continue to make their required visits to our stores, but the discussion was always about "checklist" items such as store cleanliness and proper uniforms. Attempts to discuss more important items like how best to manage inventory were met with polite nods, and then it was on to the next checklist item. The most important parts of the business did not interest them.

At the same time, sales growth at Blockbuster was beginning to slow, and Huizenga was already planning his exit. By opening 3,000 stores in six years, he had filled a demand vacuum at lightning speed. But now, the easy growth was over, and ventures into other businesses like music were not going well. Just four years later, after multiple leadership changes and the rise of Hollywood Video, Blockbuster fell from a company making so much money it couldn't spend it all to one losing money—*ten years before Netflix began streaming movies on the internet.*

For another decade, venturing out to the video store would remain America's favorite way to watch movies. Yet the industry leader, Blockbuster, was already crumbling on the inside, incapable of transforming itself from a growth company to an operating company. But before the extent of the carnage was known to the outside world, Huizenga had sold Blockbuster and was on to his next venture. The problems were left for others to fix, and that did not go well.

CHAPTER 5

THE DECLINE BEGINS

"I knew that Blockbuster was facing catastrophe and was bringing Viacom down with it."

—SUMNER REDSTONE, VIACOM CHAIRMAN

Wayne Huizenga had bought and sold hundreds of companies, but Blockbuster had turned out to be the biggest, even bigger than Waste Management. In 1994, Blockbuster had become Hollywood's largest source of revenue, and Huizenga was now one of the most powerful figures in the entertainment industry. And it would be another *fifteen years* before Netflix's streaming business would finally begin to displace video rental as the dominant way to watch movies at home.

Blockbuster stores were cash-generating machines, and still, there were no brick-and-mortar competitors large enough to threaten its dominance. But same-store sales growth had slowed (stores open more than one year), and there were not enough new store opportunities to profitably deploy Blockbuster's pile of cash.

Early results from its new ventures like music stores and amphi-theaters were not encouraging. But Wall Street looked favorably on Blockbuster's apparent transformation into an entertainment conglomerate, and its stock was trading at an all-time high.

Huizenga could have accepted his newfound stature in the enter-tainment industry and led Blockbuster to whatever came next in home entertainment. Everyone knew video stores would eventu-ally give way to some type of electronic delivery, and Blockbuster had the power and the money to lead the way. But that did not pique Huizenga's interest. The runaway growth was over, and he sensed now might be the right time to cash in and move on to the next big opportunity—to keep *building* something, not oper-ating it. As a Wall Street analyst put it: "...one of his [Huizenga's] talents was knowing when to fold 'em."[18] And like a gift from heaven, a bidding war for a Hollywood studio had created the perfect opportunity.

As Sumner Redstone, Chairman of Viacom, so aptly described the situation: "I needed cash...and Blockbuster had it."[19] For the past several months, Redstone had been locked in a bidding war with Barry Diller, the Chairman of QVC Network, Inc., for Para-mount Pictures. Viacom owned radio and television stations and a collection of cable television networks that included Showtime, MTV, Comedy Channel, and Nickelodeon. But they did not own a major studio, and Redstone craved one. The acquisition of Para-mount would vault Viacom to the ranks of the other legacy studio companies like Warner Brothers, Disney, Columbia, Universal, and 20th Century Fox.

Huizenga and Redstone joined forces and pushed for a merger of the two companies. Although there was significant dissent from the shareholders of both, the merger was completed in 1994. The deal was valued at $8.4 billion, of which Huizenga's share was about $600 million. Subsequently, Redstone got the ultimate prize he sought when Viacom completed its purchase of Paramount Pictures for $8.3 billion. Huizenga and Redstone had both gotten exactly what they wanted.

Huizenga and his partners had turned an $18.5 million investment to buy Blockbuster from David Cook into a company worth $8.4 billion—in only eight years! He had made riches for himself and thousands of others. Huizenga stayed on for a few months as co-chairman of Viacom but left shortly after the merger to launch yet another new business, AutoNation.

Blockbuster's merger with Viacom was not only an opportunity for Huizenga and shareholders to cash out; it also appeared to be a synergistic merger of complementary entertainment businesses. Viacom had added to its portfolio a major Hollywood studio in Paramount Pictures, plus the dominant force in home entertainment, Blockbuster. But that was not the reason Redstone bought Blockbuster. He did it for Blockbuster's ongoing cash flow stream. Like he said: "We needed cash...and Blockbuster had it." But not for long. Soon after the merger was completed, Blockbuster's cash flow collapsed, taking Viacom's share price with it.

Viacom's plan called for Blockbuster to generate $3 billion in free cash flow over the next five years. To be clear, that was $3 billion *after* funding thousands of new stores and other capital expenditures. As expected, Blockbuster got the "new store" part of the plan right. Even with Huizenga gone, the one thing Blockbuster knew how to do was open stores. It was its reason for existence. Over the next three years, Blockbuster *accelerated* the rate of new store growth and opened another 2,000.

That would all be great if those stores were adding to company profits, but they were not. All they were doing was adding costly overhead. Blockbuster's total failure to transition from a growth company to an operating company had been fully exposed. By 1997, Blockbuster was not generating enough cash to fund the cost of new stores and was cash-flow negative. In one of the most notable collapses in the history of American business, Blockbuster had deteriorated from a company generating more cash than it could spend to one that was opening more stores than it could pay for—in just three years.

Blockbuster had not been the unfortunate victim of an unexpected industry downturn. The video rental business was as healthy as ever and would be for more than another decade. Blockbuster's lack of attention to managing the details of its business had finally caught up with it. Simply opening more stores was no longer the answer. As one observer put it in 1997: "I have never been privy to such a drastic and immediate change as what happened at Blockbuster."[20] How did that happen?

Redstone knew Huizenga wouldn't be sticking around to run Blockbuster after the merger but had full confidence in Steve Berrard, who would replace him. Berrard was Blockbuster's CEO and had been Huizenga's right-hand man for the past decade. Redstone believed Berrard to be extremely competent and assumed there would be a seamless transition. And he was right. Under Berrard's leadership, Blockbuster continued to do exactly what it had been doing the past eight years under Huizenga's: they opened stores, ignored competition, and increasingly misjudged the evolving tastes of movie renters. It was at about this time that Nigel Travis joined Blockbuster to run its European stores. He observed the same: "Blockbuster was in disarray in Europe...no coherent strategy beyond the incessant opening of new stores. I suspected the same was true in the U.S."[21]

Soon, Redstone understood what Blockbuster *really* was. "They are deal guys. Consolidators. Huizenga and his managers were great builders but far from excellent operators," Redstone observed in retrospect. "Such a premium had been put on simply opening new stores that all controls had fallen away."[22] As details of the disaster began to trickle out to Wall Street, Viacom stock cratered. "Blockbuster was bought for the purpose of generating cash flow. Of course, the cash flow never happened," said one analyst.[23] Of Viacom's long list of assets, many analysts now valued Blockbuster at close to zero, just two years after Viacom acquired it for $8.4 billion!

Redstone knew he did not know the Blockbuster business, so he had given Berrard broad autonomy to run the company as he saw fit. But problems began surfacing almost immediately after the merger and only got worse. Two years later, Berrard left Blockbuster to rejoin Huizenga at AutoNation as its CEO. In apparent denial of the ongoing collapse of the company, Berrard proclaimed the year he left "Blockbuster's best ever." That could only mean Blockbuster had more stores than ever—which it did. But nothing else was going well.

Would this collapse have happened had Huizenga stayed on

to run Blockbuster after the merger instead of Berrard? The answer is almost assuredly, "Yes." Berrard was simply carrying out exactly what his mentor had started. At some point in the history of Blockbuster, the answer to every problem could not be to simply open more stores. That time had come, and Berrard seemed incapable of changing course. The same would have been the case had Huizenga still been running the company.

By the time Berrard left Blockbuster, Hollywood Video's strategy of locating stores across the street had produced devastating results. They had opened over 500 stores, and almost every one of them targeted a high-volume Blockbuster store. But still, Blockbuster had done nothing to answer the challenge. As a result, just two years after Viacom's acquisition of Blockbuster, Hollywood had slashed its cash flow by over $100 million and was opening a new store almost every day.

Even as store performance plummeted, Blockbuster opened even more of them—faster than ever. In 1996, they opened 804, the most of any year in the entire history of the company. Sales were increasing due to the company's obsessive drive to open more stores, but profits were declining as expenses to run all those stores increased faster than sales. It was a recipe for disaster, and that is exactly what happened.

Viacom was under assault from Wall Street and the business press. Blockbuster was leaderless, and financial performance was getting worse by the day. Redstone knew he needed a splashy hire—quick.

It had become more and more evident that Blockbuster had an

operations problem. How else could the dominant brand in home entertainment decline so much, so fast? It needed an accomplished operator—preferably a *retail* operator to turn the ship around. So, it seemed perfectly logical that Redstone would go after the most sought-after retail executive in the country—Bill Fields, the number 2 in charge and heir apparent to the CEO position at Walmart, the largest retailer in the world.

Redstone was told he could never convince Fields to come to Blockbuster, which only made him more committed to doing so. Fields became Blockbuster's third CEO in 1996, and Wall Street heralded his hiring as exactly what Blockbuster needed—a nuts-and-bolts retailer. Some even believed he was the likely successor to Redstone, who was 73 years old.

Years later, Redstone would acknowledge his misgivings about Fields. They did not "click on a personal level." But he hired him anyway because there was no question Fields was an accomplished retail operator of the highest degree—something Blockbuster had never had. To Redstone, Fields "seemed like God's gift to Blockbuster."[24] Certainly, since things had gotten so bad, it could use divine intervention.

I couldn't wait to meet Bill Fields. I had followed the rise of Walmart closely, beginning while at H-E-B, when they opened their first store in the area. Sam Walton had transformed retail, and Fields had been there almost every step of the way. Walmart had taken so much cost out of its supply chain that it could profitably sell products cheaper than anyone else. It put a lot of less efficient retailers out of business, for which it was widely criticized. But single-handedly, Walmart had raised the standard of living for millions by giving them access to products they couldn't afford previously. In the process, Walmart raised the bar for all retailers. Those who did not acknowledge that—Sears, for example—are gone. Those who did—H-E-B, for example—became better companies by learning from Walmart.

Bill Fields had been at Walmart throughout the company's rise to dominance. When Sumner Redstone contacted him in 1996, he was an Executive Vice President and President and CEO of the store division, which was then a $68 billion business. He was in line for the top job at Walmart, yet Redstone had convinced him to join Blockbuster. For a retail junkie like me, who had watched Blockbuster ignore its store operations for so long, it did not get any better than this. Fields had recently told a meeting of analysts that his plans would increase cash flow 15 to 20 percent in the next two years. I couldn't wait to hear more.

That opportunity came when he attended a Franchise Advisory Council (FAC) meeting, the first CEO to do so in the past several years. The FAC was a council of franchisees meant to be a liaison with Blockbuster. It had no official power but served a useful purpose by discussing important issues with company executives in a small setting. I had been a member of the council since 1994, and we were all excited Fields had chosen to meet with us because Huizenga and Berrard never did.

Fields had been with Blockbuster for just a few weeks and was still getting acclimated to a business that was nothing like Walmart. Most of his comments were general. He indicated he would be looking at new products to sell in the stores, negotiating better deals with suppliers, streamlining operations, etc. It was early, so his comments included few details. But two things stood out. He never asked us what we thought had gone wrong with Blockbuster, and he hardly mentioned Blockbuster's primary business—renting movies. That seemed odd since he had no experience renting movies, and we did. And, more importantly, franchise stores were outperforming corporate stores by a wide margin for the first time in company history. Didn't he want to know why? But like all his predecessors at Blockbuster, he didn't care what franchisees thought. More alarming, though, renting movies did not seem to be on his radar.

During a break, I got a chance to introduce myself and ask the new CEO a few questions. Fields, of course, knew of and respected H-E-B, so that was a good entrée. Since he had hardly mentioned the rental business in his remarks, I asked him what he thought about it. I was shocked at his answer: "I think it's dead!" he said. My next question should have been: "Then why are you opening another 700 stores this year?" But I was so startled by the comment, I did not have the wherewithal to ask. I later learned that he told a group of corporate executives that Blockbuster would never have another year of same-store sales growth in rentals. It was becoming obvious Fields had not come to Blockbuster to embrace and grow the rental business. He had come to transform it into something else entirely.

Fields did not want input from franchisees or even corporate executives who had been in the business for up to ten years. Nigel Travis tells the story in his book *The Challenge Culture* about an offsite strategy session in which Fields revealed his five strategy points and asked for feedback. No one volunteered any because it did not seem he particularly wanted it, so he moved on. Those five points became the strategy for Blockbuster going forward.[25]

Perhaps Field's strategy was best revealed when he removed "Video" from "Blockbuster Video." From that point forward, the famous blue and gold ticket would say simply "Blockbuster." Then he dumped "Make It a Blockbuster Night," the company slogan of the past few years, and replaced it with "One World, One Word: Blockbuster." Evidently, he really did believe video rental was dead, just as he had told me. No one had a clue what the new slogan meant. But Fields' view of the business had become totally clear. He believed rental was dying and must be replaced with (fill in the blank).

Fields shrunk the space devoted to rental in stores and replaced it with music CDs, books, magazines, clothing, video games, computer software, stuffed animals, trinkets of all kinds—anything but movies for rent. It would have been comical had it not been so tragic. Anyone who had been in the business for long knew this stuff would not sell. Most of us had already tried—repeatedly. Yet here was this legendary retailer from Walmart to prove us all wrong. In short, sales tanked, and stores were stuck with a bunch of junk no one would buy. But Fields was just getting started.

As if Blockbuster had not sunk enough cash into unproductive stores, Fields decided to spend even more to move the corporate office from Ft. Lauderdale to Dallas, Texas. There didn't seem to be a good reason, other than Fields wanted to get out from under the shadow of the now legendary Wayne Huizenga, who still lived and officed there. Much of the senior management team and support staff refused to move to Dallas and resigned.

Given what Fields thought of the video rental business, that may have been by design.

Fields then made plans to open a state-of-the-art, 800,000 square foot distribution center to ship stores all the merchandise that would not sell. It was also used for rental products but was not nearly as efficient as several companies that specialized in video distribution and who had spent years perfecting it, companies like Ingram Distributing and Video Products Distributors (VPD).

It is not an exaggeration to say that *nothing* Fields implemented worked. Every component of his "transform Blockbuster strategy" flopped, and the company's decline steepened. Soon, Redstone had enough. By "mutual agreement," Fields was out—just 13 months after he became CEO of Blockbuster. He never saw the new headquarters in Dallas or his prized distribution center. Instead, Blockbuster took a $250 million inventory write-down for all the stuff we knew would not sell and was in worse financial condition than ever. God's gift to Blockbuster Fields was not.

The situation was so dire that Sumner Redstone decided to take things into his own hands. He even made plans to attend the next FAC meeting with franchisees. He wanted to know what we thought about the business, and we certainly wanted to know his views because the cash cow he thought he'd bought was practically on life support. Redstone attended the next meeting, accompanied by his first lieutenant, Tom Dooley. In contrast to the conciliatory remarks made publicly when Fields left by "mutual agreement," Redstone opened the meeting with a scathing rebuke of everything Fields did in his short time at

Blockbuster. He described the Blockbuster distribution center as being jammed with stuffed animals, T-shirts, and all kinds of other "crap" that would never sell. He wished he had fired Fields sooner. He said he was looking for a new CEO, but in the meantime, *he* would be running things. He was, in fact, spending several days a week at the new headquarters in downtown Dallas, which he called a "total wasteland."[26]

In short, Redstone was livid. Blockbuster was going down and taking Viacom with it. Viacom's stock had dropped so much that key executives were leaving because their stock options were underwater. Redstone blamed the entire debacle on Blockbuster. His remarks in that meeting stunned the members of the FAC. The situation was much worse than we thought. Three years after the merger, what was left of the Blockbuster management team was demoralized. Two CEOs had left the company, as well as most senior management. Blockbuster was a shell of its former self, and there was no clear road to recovery.

But the FAC meeting with Redstone was not an open discussion about what was wrong with Blockbuster. It was much more about what *he* thought. We would have liked to have told him that, unlike his stores, our business was actually pretty good. Like Blockbuster, most of us were competing against the new Hollywood Video stores, but we had employed different strategies to compete and were getting much better results. We could have had a productive discussion about how and why, but that did not happen.

Redstone was a Hollywood mogul and did not understand the video rental business well enough to discuss what really mattered, but until he found a new CEO, *he* would be running the company. The meeting had been mostly about how Blockbuster was killing Viacom, not what the franchisees thought could be done to fix it. We never got the impression Redstone was interested in what we thought, and he never met with the franchisees again.

To the general public, it must have appeared nothing had changed since Viacom bought Blockbuster. Every year, hundreds of new Blockbuster stores continued to open all over the country. And it had expanded its international presence with thousands of new stores in the United Kingdom, Brazil, Mexico, Australia, and other countries all over the world.

The Blockbuster brand had continued to grow. There was a Blockbuster Bowl football game. A Blockbuster blimp. A Blockbuster credit card. There was even a Blockbuster Entertainment Awards show that stood for years alongside the Oscars and the Emmys. And Blockbuster continued to be the only video company with a national advertising presence. On the surface, it must have appeared to most that Blockbuster was as dominant as ever.

Even to franchisees, the full extent of the carnage was not clear. Blockbuster shared a variety of store metrics with franchisees, and we could see the decline in important statistics like average store sales, customer visits, and other crucial data. To those on the inside, the decline was obvious, but we did not have visibility to all the company numbers. So, as the truth trickled out each quarter, we were all surprised by how bad it had become.

Although still dominant in 1996 because of its sheer size, Blockbuster was in trouble financially. In a stunning decline, average annual store sales in the U.S. had fallen over 20 percent from $900,000 to $700,000 over the last three years. Sales growth had not kept pace with new store openings, which, given the high fixed costs of the business, virtually guaranteed the financial problems that would plague Blockbuster for years to come.

This dramatic decline occurred years before new technologies would pose legitimate threats. Years before internet-delivered video. Years before Netflix by-mail, and even more before Netflix streaming. Years before Redbox. And even years before the now ubiquitous Digital Video Recorder (DVR). Technology had *nothing* to do with Blockbuster's three-year fall from a company with more cash than it could spend to being cash poor. The truth is, Wayne Huizenga and Steve Berrard did not know much about the video rental business, other than how to open thousands of stores against mostly small and undercapitalized competitors. And while they could have learned a lot from the good ones, like Video Central and others, they arrogantly chose to ignore them.

Unknowingly, Sumner Redstone had bought a company in 1994 that was on the verge of collapse. Blockbuster had been built to grow and nothing else. He didn't know how to fix it, and Bill Fields certainly didn't either. Would the next Blockbuster CEO please step forward?

THE LEGEND OF WAYNE HUIZENGA

This chapter closes the story of Wayne Huizenga's time with Blockbuster. I, along with all the other franchisees, have often wondered—what would have happened had he not sold the company to Viacom and instead stayed on to run it through those difficult years in the mid-1990s? Had Viacom not so desperately needed Blockbuster's cash to buy Paramount, it is unlikely Huizenga would have ever been offered a price close to the $8.4 billion. Had that been the case, he may have never sold it. That wouldn't have changed the fact that Blockbuster was so ill-prepared to deal with a maturing, more competitive industry. But what would have happened had Huizenga been in charge during those difficult years instead of Steve Berrard, Sumner Redstone, and Bill Fields?

Huizenga spent ten years building Waste Management into the largest waste company in the world. He left that company almost 40 years ago, and it is *still* the largest waste company in the world. Immediately after leaving Blockbuster, he founded AutoNation and, after some early difficulties, hired Mike Jackson to manage what is still the largest auto dealership in the country. Jackson remains its Executive Chairman and is considered the voice of the entire auto dealership industry.

Those three companies—Blockbuster, Waste Management, and AutoNation—were all Fortune 500 companies. Huizenga is the only person in history to have built three of them. He had similar success with his professional sports franchises. He brought professional baseball to Florida in 1993, and the Marlins won the World Series in 1997, just four years later. He brought professional hockey to Florida in 1992, and the Panthers reached the Stanley Cup Finals in just four years.

He bought the Miami Dolphins, and had their head coach Nick Saban not been lured away by the University of Alabama, they may have won a few Super Bowls. Yes, *that* Nick Saban. Huizenga recruited him away from LSU in 2005 to coach the Dolphins, but he left for Alabama just two years later. Although their professional relationship was brief, Saban revered Huizenga. When Huizenga passed away in March 2018, he recalled his time with Huizenga: "There is no one I know, other than my parents, that is someone I'd more like to emulate than Wayne Huizenga. The way he treated other people, the class that he had, the intelligence—he was the classiest man you're ever going to meet."[27]

Most Blockbuster franchisees have equally fond memories of Wayne Huizenga. It seemed everything he touched turned to gold, and they got to share in it. So, most like to believe that had he still been there in 1995 when Blockbuster began to face huge challenges, Huizenga would have found a way to weather the storm. But I believe the facts suggest otherwise.

By opening 3,000 Blockbuster stores in just seven years, Wayne Huizenga brilliantly filled a void in an industry that had been built by undercapitalized entrepreneurs. But soon after he left, it became clear he had not built a company that could effectively manage thousands of small retail stores in an increasingly competitive environment. It was nothing like overseeing a fleet of garbage trucks or a chain of auto dealerships.

Huizenga said over and over that he was driven to build companies, not to run them, and he tried to fill that void at Blockbuster by hiring accomplished retail professionals. But none had the *authority* to change the culture Huizenga had created. The same was true of Blockbuster Music, Discovery Zone, and the other retail companies he formed under the Blockbuster umbrella, all of which failed. For long-term survival, Blockbuster required an accomplished retail executive with authority to build a nimble, competent organization with an eye on the future. But in the eight years that Huizenga presided over Blockbuster, that never happened. It is difficult to envision that changing in subsequent years.

There is one thing we can all agree on, though. Had Huizenga been at Blockbuster in 2000 when Reed Hastings offered to sell Netflix to Blockbuster for $50 million, he would have "damn sure" bought it—but for a lot less after he finished negotiating. And he would have convinced Hastings to take a pay cut to come to work for him!

CHAPTER 6

ORDER RESTORED?

"...throughout my career, I'd been successful by defying the status quo at important junctures and that's what I thought had to be done in this case."

—JOHN ANTIOCO, CHAIRMAN AND CEO
OF BLOCKBUSTER, 1997-2007[28]

It is 1997, the year the story of Blockbuster and the history of home entertainment would begin to be rewritten. It is the year the Digital Video Disc (DVD) is introduced to replace the clunky, inconvenient VHS videocassette. It is also the year a couple of Silicon Valley entrepreneurs named Reed Hastings and Marc Randolph start a company to mail those DVDs to customers through the postal service. They considered dozens of names for their new company and eventually settled on *Netflix*, even though they feared it was a little "porny" because it sounded too much like "skinflix."[29] And that same year, John Antioco joined Blockbuster as CEO to try to save it from itself.

DVD was about to change everything about home entertainment; the business Blockbuster had brought mainstream and now dominated. But three years after Viacom bought the company, it was in disarray and in no position to manage through such a momentous change. The transition from VHS to DVD over the next few years would be revolutionary, and the fate of the company would rest on the critical decisions required to navigate it. But by whom? Blockbuster was leaderless and cash poor. For a while, it appeared John Antioco was perfect to lead Blockbuster into the new world created by DVD. But a few years later, Blockbuster was again struggling to survive. It is said that history is written by the victors, and from this point forward, the history of home entertainment would be written by Netflix, the little company that started the same year John Antioco joined Blockbuster.

To a struggling company starving for competent leadership, John Antioco seemed the perfect answer. He attended a national franchise meeting shortly after joining Blockbuster and masterfully worked the crowd—smiling, engaging, asking all the right questions. And unlike any of his predecessors, he listened to what we had to say and seemed to understand. When he spoke to the gathering for the first time, he commanded the stage. He was new to the business but already spoke more eloquently about it than any of his predecessors. There was not one person in the room who did not believe Antioco was the right person to bring Blockbuster back from the brink of failure in 1997.

We heard the same about his impact at corporate headquarters. "Will this company fail?" a fired-up Antioco asked in a meeting. "Not on my watch. No way, no how."[30] It is remarkable that in 1997, there was concern that Blockbuster *could* fail, but that is how bad things had become. Antioco addressed the issue head-on and with a confidence that revitalized the entire company. He was developing a plan to bring Blockbuster back from the brink, and we all got the sense that he could and would.

Wall Street was not as confident. The Viacom/Blockbuster merger had been a disaster, and investors had lost confidence in Blockbuster's leadership and Sumner Redstone's ability to fix it. Legendary investor Mario Gabelli, one of Viacom's largest shareholders, summed up what many believed. "It was a mistake [for Viacom] to make the acquisition [in 1994], and it's [still] a mistake. The growth potential just isn't there."[31] Antioco skillfully used this widespread skepticism to fire up the troops even more. It was Blockbuster against the world!

Like Bill Fields, all Antioco's experience was in retail, but unlike the giant stores Fields ran at Walmart, all Antioco's experience was with smaller stores. He began his career as a trainee with 7-Eleven in 1970 and rose quickly through the ranks, holding several senior management positions, including VP of Operations for the 7,000-store chain. After 20 years with 7-Eleven, he left to become Chief Operating Officer at Pearle Vision, a retail eyeglass chain. Two years later, he joined Circle K convenience stores as Chief Operating Officer and later became Chairman and CEO. While at Circle K, he led the company out of Chapter 11 bankruptcy, organized a management buyout, and eventually took the company public in 1995.

But it was his short stint as President and CEO of Taco Bell that got Sumner Redstone's attention and is the reason he hired him. Taco Bell was struggling when Antioco arrived, but he engineered a drastic turnaround in less than a year. Roger Enrico, CEO of PepsiCo, which was the owner of Taco Bell at the time, called Antioco "a gifted executive who had done an extraordinary job in his brief time at Taco Bell."[32] At age 47, Antioco had already built a well-deserved reputation as a turnaround artist, and all his experience was in small retail. Although he had no experience in home entertainment, he had excelled in a wide range of retail businesses. There was no reason to believe his skills were not adaptable to Blockbuster.

Unlike all his predecessors, Antioco engaged franchisees. Soon after he joined Blockbuster, he played golf with me at a franchise function, something prior CEOs would have never done. After years of trying to engage Blockbuster executives in discussions about the business, what came next was a welcome change. Antioco and I had the most in-depth discussion I had ever had with a Blockbuster executive, and he seemed interested in what I thought. The topics were wide-ranging and, eventually, Hollywood Video came up, which by now had over 800 stores. I explained that Hollywood Video had already opened six stores in El Paso against our ten, and more were on the way. I was pleasantly surprised when he asked what he could do to help. We were paying Blockbuster over $1.5 million a year in franchise royalties and fees. So, I suggested that we divert some of that money to advertising and extra product to fight our new competitor. He agreed to a $250,000 package, which helped us reverse our negative sales trends.

Antioco's outreach to the franchise community continued when he agreed to the formation of a franchise association managed by franchisees instead of Blockbuster. The Franchise Advisory

Council (FAC) had been in place since the beginning, but its entire agenda was driven by Blockbuster, not franchisees. Scott Watson, Blockbuster's first international franchisee with stores in Alberta, Canada, as well as several in Shreveport, Louisiana, had tried for years to organize franchise-led meetings so we could set our own agenda of discussion topics. But Blockbuster did not want us to organize and blocked all his attempts to meet independently of them. They even refused to provide a contact list of all the franchisees.

But with the change in leadership, Watson saw an opportunity for positive change and asked Antioco if he would support an association that would be managed entirely by franchisees. He agreed on the spot, and the Association of Blockbuster Franchisees (ABF) was formed. The FAC was disbanded, and the ABF became the primary liaison between Blockbuster and franchisees. Watson headed the ABF as President and added two more professionals as support. The organization was funded by dues from franchisees and was completely independent of Blockbuster. The ABF was managed by a board of directors elected by franchisees, of which I was a member until it disbanded in 2014, four years after Blockbuster filed bankruptcy.

The ABF represented a complete reversal in the way Blockbuster had interacted with franchisees for the past ten years. Instead of carefully orchestrated meetings that were planned entirely by Blockbuster, all future meetings would be planned and managed by the staff of the ABF. In addition, the ABF board met quarterly with top Blockbuster executives and more often when necessary. The board formed a strong working relationship with Nigel Travis, who was by now number two in charge behind Antioco.

We were disappointed that John Antioco never attended the ABF board meetings, which was a precursor of things to come. But the board always had a constructive working relationship with Travis and later his replacement, Nick Shepherd. Thousands of hours were spent hashing out franchisor/franchisee challenges in meetings of the board, committees, and task forces. Virtually every critical decision Blockbuster made affected franchisees, and those decisions were openly debated in countless meetings that are the foundation for much of this book.

The introduction of DVD began slowly, with studios releasing a few titles at a time. It would be another year before Blockbuster would need to decide exactly how to adopt this new technology. In the interim, Antioco needed to engineer a turnaround with VHS movies while positioning the company for the transition to come. He hit the ground running, and the changes were quick and decisive.

Since its founding in 1985, every new Blockbuster store was essentially the same as the last, except for prices, which had only gone up. While competitors were using lower prices to steal its customers, the price for renting movies at Blockbuster was higher than ever. Hollywood Video now had over 800 stores, and every one of them had larger inventories and lower prices than Blockbuster. It was the main reason Hollywood Video generated more sales per store and had devastated every Blockbuster store against which it competed.

All Antioco's predecessors believed lower prices meant lower sales and had done nothing to counter the attack from Holly-wood Video and other smaller competitors. It demonstrated an astonishing misunderstanding of the basic principles of retail management. Even Bill Fields, who spent 20 years with Walmart, the king of low prices, did nothing to fix this price discrepancy. From its beginning, all Blockbuster's leaders had ignorantly believed that just being Blockbuster was enough and did nothing as competitors used lower prices to steal millions of customers. When Antioco surveyed the situation and decided what needed to be done, he must have thought, "This is too easy!"

John Antioco had a reputation for being focused on the customer. He had also been around retailing long enough to know that a store cannot allow a competitor across the street to sell the exact same thing for less than half the price. Video rental was essentially a commodity business. Every store was renting the exact same movies. Other variables, such as location and customer service, were essentially the same among the larger video stores of the day. In the case of Hollywood Video, its stores were usually bigger, well located, and customer service was comparable to Blockbuster stores. There were no discernible differences other than prices.

The fix was obvious to an experienced retailer like Antioco, and his first move was to match Hollywood Video's prices and, in many cases, undercut them. And exactly as happened five years before when we lowered prices in our Alaska and El Paso stores, Blockbuster sales trends immediately improved. By simply following an elementary principle of retailing, Antioco had reversed the negative sales trends of the dominant force in home entertainment.

Antioco's most drastic price cut came in the catalog section.

Although every indicator screamed old movies were worth less than new ones, Blockbuster had never gotten the message. By now, even most franchisees had reduced catalog prices. But when Antioco arrived, Blockbuster was the *only* video rental chain in the country that still charged the same price for catalog movies as new releases. The company had disconnected itself from reality, and Antioco brought it back. The results were astonishing, with double-digit sales increases almost overnight. Finally, a Blockbuster CEO that got it.

Next, Antioco addressed the problem that had plagued Blockbuster for years: its poor availability of new releases, which he termed "managed dissatisfaction." Because of the $65 price for most new releases, this problem was inherent to the business. No video store could stay in stock *all* the time. But Blockbuster's archaic and elementary management systems had made the problem much worse than it should have been. This had been demonstrated for years by the buying recommendations they sent franchisees every week, most of which were never looked at and thrown in the trash. They were irrelevant, and from the dismal in-stock condition in Blockbuster's own stores, they must have been using the same archaic system.

Franchisees became so frustrated with the outdated management system, we formally requested that Blockbuster commit to upgrading it. If not for them, at least for us. For the first time since Blockbuster's founding over ten years before, they agreed to upgrade the inventory management system for franchisees. It came to be known as the Franchise Back-Office Management System (FBOS). They committed a small group of programmers to the project, and franchisees would provide the specifications.

Using raw data files, we had already built an inventory management system for our company's stores that was more advanced than Blockbuster's, so we happily volunteered to provide most of the specifications for FBOS. Mark Merriam, our company's product manager, spent countless hours with Blockbuster programmers detailing what the system needed, and it was launched about two years later. It was an extremely effective tool franchisees used to better manage their inventory, which was unquestionably the most difficult but also the most important part of managing a Blockbuster store. FBOS was so effective, we soon learned of envious Blockbuster corporate associates who believed it was far better than the systems they used, which was a testament to how little attention Blockbuster paid to the most important component of the business—managing the product.

The management system Antioco inherited from his predecessors was an embarrassment for a company of Blockbuster's size. They had the resources to fix it but never did. They never seemed to understand how a 5 percent improvement in buying accuracy could save the company hundreds of millions of dollars and, better yet, improve in-stock conditions and satisfy millions more customers. Blockbuster never managed the business at that level of detail. It had made some improvements since Wayne Huizenga told Steve Berrard to visit the stores on Saturday night to count movies but not much.

Instead of fixing the management systems that created Blockbuster's in-stock problems, Antioco decided to flood the stores with new releases on a program called *revenue sharing*. It had been around for years, but few used it because it did not work. In fact, the person who pioneered the idea built one of the early video store chains, but it failed early on.

So exactly what was revenue sharing? It is a crucial part of this story because it became a drug Blockbuster could never kick; the addiction persisted all the way to bankruptcy a decade later.

Revenue sharing was a means by which studios charged Blockbuster more for a movie title by selling them more copies at a lower price per copy. For example, Studio A would sell Blockbuster 100 copies of a movie for $65 per copy for a total cost of $6,500. Or it would sell Blockbuster 300 units for $30 a copy for a total cost of $9,000. The intent was to increase total store sales because the stores had more copies. But if that did not happen, profit declined because of the higher cost to buy movies.

Studios varied in their approach to revenue sharing, but the typical deal would look something like this: Blockbuster pays $7 a copy to get those 300 units in the store. Each unit generates $57 in sales, and Blockbuster pays 40 percent of that to the studio, about $23. The total cost of each unit, therefore, is $30—$7 up front plus $23 in "shared revenue." The details of each deal varied by studio, but the basic approach was the same. Some studios even required "minimums," meaning that even if a title did not rent enough to generate $23 per copy in "shared revenue," Blockbuster owed it anyway.

To "sweeten" the deal for Blockbuster, the "shared revenue" portion was usually paid out over six months as opposed to the 60-day payment terms if the movie was bought outright for $65. These extended terms added to the addictive high and made it extremely costly to kick the habit. As Blockbuster's cash problems mounted a few years later, this weakened their negotiating position. The studios had become the drug "pusher." Blockbuster had to have the movies sold by the pusher, but more and more, it would be on terms more favorable to the studios than Blockbuster.

To make matters even worse, almost all revenue sharing programs required Blockbuster to purchase a certain number of movies that were known as "B" titles. These were called "output" deals, meaning that Blockbuster was required to buy every title the studios "put out," good or bad. "B" titles were movies that either failed at theaters or were never meant to be there in the first place. Some were good and added to the reason people went to video stores—to find those "sleepers," available nowhere else. But a lot of "B" movies were terribly made and not worth the price of the video cassette they came in. In fact, Blockbuster's output revenue sharing programs helped fund hundreds of independent films over the years that otherwise would have never been made. Some of those movies were good for the world and good for Blockbuster. Many were not. But on revenue sharing, Blockbuster did not get the right to choose between the winners and the losers. They got them all.

The fact is, there was not much "*sharing*" in "revenue sharing." The fixed costs were very high. If more copies did not generate more sales, profit declined. The common theme of *every* revenue-sharing deal ever created was higher costs. There were no exceptions to that rule.

The flood of more copies of movies on revenue sharing deals did help correct the "managed dissatisfaction" problem Antioco spoke of. But it covered up the deficient management systems that caused the problem in the first place. The company came to rely on the massive quantities supplied from revenue-sharing deals to cover up serious inefficiencies. In a few years, when it needed to get off revenue sharing in order to save the company, it didn't know how. Blockbuster was hopelessly addicted.

The way Antioco and Sumner Redstone sold the revenue-sharing program was the first sign that something was amiss. Both got very loose with the facts, and I started to get concerned.

Redstone led the way when he claimed Blockbuster "created" revenue sharing and "changed this industry."[33] That was never the case. He went on to claim that because Blockbuster paid $65 to buy movies, it cost $650,000 to stock every new store.[34] That was even less true. Blockbuster was paying about one-third of that to buy the inventory to stock new stores because older movies, which comprised about three-fourths of the inventory, cost as little as $8. And by now, more and more new releases cost much less than $65 through quantity discount programs. Plus, more and more titles were being released at direct-to-consumer prices for about $20 wholesale—all kids movies and many big box-office titles. The industry had changed a lot from the early days when all new releases really did cost about $65. But that was ten years before. The average price in 1997 had fallen to around $40. Redstone did not seem to understand that and continued to peddle a totally fake story that Blockbuster had saved the business from $65 movies.

Antioco was more understated in his comments but proudly wore the title of the one who had saved Blockbuster with revenue-sharing deals that were won in hard-fought negotiations with the studios. But revenue sharing wasn't "saving" anything—I know, I tried it.

When Antioco was launching his revenue-sharing strategy, he called me and several other franchisees and asked us to participate. Even though we had developed our own effective ways to buy new releases, I wanted to cooperate with the new CEO and agreed to try it on a six-month test. Not surprisingly, the terms of the deal were similar to what had existed for many years. I knew it would be expensive, but I thought it was worth trying, particularly since Blockbuster would be backing it up with their new "Go Home Happy" national advertising campaign. If we could increase sales enough to just break even, it would be worth it. Unfortunately for us, that did not happen. Although Blockbuster enjoyed a double-digit improvement in sales by covering up its ineffective buying systems, it couldn't fix problems our stores did not have, and our sales never moved. The test cost us about $600,000 in higher cost for product. Lesson learned. We got off the drug after the six-month test.

For many of Blockbuster's smaller competitors, however, revenue sharing had awakened the sleeping giant. Suddenly, those empty new release shelves at Blockbuster on Saturday night were full again with movies to rent, and customers were flocking to them. To fight back, a group of independent video store owners filed a lawsuit against the studios claiming unfair trade practice. They were convinced Blockbuster was getting exclusive, low-cost revenue-sharing deals not available to them. Many had tried revenue sharing and found it prohibitively expensive. Blockbuster must be getting a better deal, they thought.

But court proceedings have a way of uncovering the truth, and this trial revealed the myth Blockbuster had created about revenue sharing. Antioco and Redstone had not negotiated anything unusual. They had not "created" revenue sharing, as Redstone claimed. They were using a system that had been around for years and was available to anyone. There was nothing exclusive about it.

"The deal offered to Blockbuster was offered to every single one of our customers," said former Universal Studios Home Video executive VP and COO William Clark.[35] Another studio executive suggested that the plaintiffs go to Rentrak, a distributor that offered similar revenue-sharing terms to those Blockbuster received. And in a reference to all the "B" movies included in output revenue-sharing deals, a Columbia Studios representative put it perfectly when she said independent store owners told her they wouldn't buy the product from Columbia at any price because it wouldn't rent. As she described it: "They weren't supporting my junk. I don't know how else to say it. I wasn't keeping it from them."[36]

After hearing testimony for a few days, the judge quickly dismissed the case for lack of evidence. The myth had been unmasked. Revenue sharing was indeed available to everyone. It had been for years. Blockbuster had used it to mask its inability to manage a fundamental of the business—its rental inventory. And it worked for a time. Sales improved, customers came back, and revenue sharing helped save Blockbuster from failure. But it came at a very high price and failed to address fundamental problems. Here are the facts.

When Viacom bought Blockbuster in 1994 for $8.4 billion, the company had 3,600 stores and was generating more than $700 million in cash flow, more than it could spend on new stores. By the time Antioco had "saved" Blockbuster, it had doubled its store count to about 7,200 stores but was still *less profitable* than when it had half as many. Antioco had saved Blockbuster from an early grave, but Blockbuster had spent over $1 billion opening more stores plus added billions more in liabilities in the form of fixed costs from store leases, insurance, taxes, payroll, and more. Over the past ten years, Blockbuster's profit margins had declined by half, and it had added billions in liabilities. It was in its weakest position ever to deal with competitive challenges to come, and it would only get worse.

Wall Street understood the situation, too. In 1999, two years after Antioco became CEO, Viacom spun off 20 percent of the company in an Initial Public Offering (IPO). The offering valued Blockbuster's equity at $2.7 billion, a 68 percent decline from the purchase price of $8.4 billion just six years before. The company had lost $6.4 billion in value even though it had *doubled* its store count. The common theme had continued: Blockbuster knew how to open stores but not much else.

Revenue sharing only worked to disguise Blockbuster's problems for a while. When sales growth began to slow a year after it was introduced, Antioco began raising prices in a desperate attempt to keep Wall Street satisfied—reversing a change to which he had attributed Blockbuster's resurgence. Lower prices had played a major role in bringing Blockbuster back from disaster, but within a few years, its rental prices were higher than ever—higher even than before Antioco came to Blockbuster. Each time he raised prices, sales would improve, but only temporarily as higher prices began driving customers away. It was a no-win, never-ending cycle that weakened the company and left it more vulnerable than ever to new competitors who were closing in.

Out of weapons, Blockbuster launched an endless series of gimmicky promotions. They created Carl and Ray—a rabbit and a guinea pig voiced by Jim Belushi and James Woods—to sell the promotions on expensive television campaigns. But no promotion could fix what Antioco had broken with his relentless march to higher prices.

When the promotions did not work, Antioco established a strategic task force to find new sources of revenue. This led to two recycled ideas, a pizza partnership with Round Table Pizza and a small electronics partnership with Radio Shack. Both were "Blockbusterized" versions of old ideas that had been tried many times before. Not surprisingly, both failed—again.

Wall Street was becoming impatient, and Blockbuster's stock price was cut in half just a few months after its IPO. But it was even worse. We could see what Wall Street could not see. Customer visits and movie rentals were falling faster than sales but were being camouflaged by higher prices—the highest in the history of the company. Customers were leaving Blockbuster in droves, and it set the stage for yet another financial calamity in the still short history of Blockbuster.

But a lifeline was developing at astonishing speed. The DVD player had become the fastest-growing electronics appliance in history. It would create an incalculable opportunity, but it would also create Netflix and Redbox. How would Antioco negotiate this rapidly changing marketplace? His decisions would define Blockbuster's future.

CHAPTER 7

DEATH BY DVD

"There's really not much reason to dither about it anymore: It is now clear that DVD is going to take over the world."

—TOM ADAMS, HOLLYWOOD AFTERMARKET, AUGUST 2000

The Digital Video Disc (DVD) made its debut in 1997 and, three years later, it was on its way to replacing the VHS videocassette as America's favorite way to watch movies. It was superior to VHS in too many ways to count. Its convenient size and superior video and audio quality were just the beginning. Viewers could skip from scene to scene or episode to episode, could change languages, turn on subtitles. The list of benefits was endless. And it forever ended that annoying plea from video stores: "Please Be Kind, Rewind." It all sounds so yesterday now, but it was revolutionary at the time.

Pay-per-view movies through cable and direct-broadcast-satellite were still a relatively small business, and it would be ten years before increased bandwidth enabled the internet to pose a threat to Blockbuster. There was a long runway for DVD to dominate home entertainment, and it did. It became the fastest-growing electronic device of all time.

But DVD was not meant to save Blockbuster. It was meant to kill it. Warren Lieberfarb, who is considered the "Father of the DVD," said as much when he told the *New York Times* in 2001 that "Blockbuster is an endangered species!"[37] Lieberfarb was the President of Warner Home Video and the driving force behind the development of the DVD. It was superior to VHS in every way, but that was not why he thought it would doom Blockbuster. The reason was the DVD's low price. This *eliminated* the "rental window," which for years had landed most VHS movies in video stores to *rent* months before they went to Walmart to *sell*.

Every DVD ever released was intended to sell directly to consumers, not to Blockbuster to rent. Gone was the $65 price no customer would pay. DVD new releases were priced at about $20 at retailers, a price Lieberfarb believed would push most people to buy instead of rent. Why *rent* it for $4 when you can *own* it for $20? Every title would be for sale at Walmart and thousands of other retailers the same day it appeared on Blockbuster shelves for rent. Blockbuster and the entire video store industry had been built on the "rental window." DVD eliminated it forever.

But anyone who had been in the video rental business since its beginning believed consumers would continue to rent more than buy, regardless of the format or the price. Customers wanted to own movies for kids and a few select new release titles made for adults—the "sell-through" titles, as we called them. *Titanic* had been the most successful of those sell-through titles for adults, but even it still rented millions of times in video stores.

Lieberfarb and many others in Hollywood believed—or perhaps hoped—that the convenient size and superior quality of DVD would eliminate Blockbuster. But John Antioco accurately pointed out that the DVD's drastically lower price was "...the best news I've heard in a long time. We can lower our price somewhat to the renter, and our margins will improve."[38] Had he followed his own advice, Blockbuster might still be here today. But instead, he did the exact opposite. No, DVD did not kill Blockbuster. Blockbuster killed Blockbuster. DVD was its weapon of choice.

Had the studios gotten their way, Blockbuster would have never existed in the first place. Many in Hollywood believed DVD was a way to right the wrong inflicted on them when the Supreme Court refused to shut the business down 15 years before. But, by now, VHS movie rentals exceeded the total sales of theater tickets and movies on VHS videocassette combined! When it came to watching movies, video rental was king. Nothing else came close. It was a way of life in America. Why on earth would the studios want to use DVD to kill something loved and preferred by so many?

There was a simple reason—math. For every $4 *rental* at Blockbuster, the studio share was about $1.50. For every $20 *sell* of a DVD at Walmart, the studio share was about $15. Every *rent* converted into a *sell* was therefore worth $13.50 more to the studios than a rental of the same movie at Blockbuster. The upside was so significant, they did not need to convert all renters into buyers. If the studios could convert only one out of every ten renters into a buyer, they would make more money, and perhaps Blockbuster would be a thing of the past.

As it turned out, Americans did love to buy DVDs, and they bought about twice as many of them as they did movies on VHS videocassette. But they loved to *rent* DVDs even more. As DVD became the dominant format, it continued to *rent three times more often than it sold*. And the cost for video stores to buy them was less than half that of movies on VHS videocassette. The opportunity to use DVD rental to increase profit and transition into electronic delivery was enormous. One company did exactly that, but it was not Blockbuster. The name of that company was Netflix, and the next chapter is the story of how they did it.

John Antioco was one who seemed to always be looking for the "silver bullet" or what some might call "lightning in a bottle." Everyone who knew him well talked about how he was all about "big ideas." "If you're going to do it, do it big!" That was John Antioco, and he would demonstrate that time and time again. But despite the tremendous success of DVD, he never viewed it as one of those "big ideas." It was imposed on him by the studios to kill Blockbuster. But the truth is, DVD was a *gift* from the studios that gave Blockbuster its best opportunity to increase profit while it learned how the home entertainment business was evolving, buying time to prepare for the eventual transition to electronically delivered movies.

DVD could have been, and *should* have been, the silver bullet Antioco so desperately wanted. The ultimate *big idea*. But as DVD was taking over the industry at the turn of the century, the typical Blockbuster store had less of what customers wanted at prices higher than they were willing to pay. How did a company as dominant as Blockbuster so underestimate smaller startup companies like Netflix and Redbox? It all started with Blockbuster's failed transition from VHS to DVD.

Blockbuster bungled the conversion to DVD on a colossal scale and in many different ways. But it all started with inventory management, which is a recurring theme throughout the story of Blockbuster. The company that had all the data could never seem to understand what customers wanted before someone else figured it out first.

This issue is best characterized by the following example. In 1998, when Antioco was bringing Blockbuster back from the dead, VHS still made up 95 percent of the video rental business. Blockbuster's catalog inventory at that time averaged 6,400 units per store, and it rented about 1,065 times per week. Six years later, in 2004, after DVD had taken over the business, Blockbuster had only 3,400 units in its catalog inventory, and it rented 538 times per week. Its inventories had been cut in *half* and, predictably, lower sales followed. Blockbuster had failed at a most basic and elementary business principle. You cannot rent what you do not have.

Blockbuster didn't rebuild its inventory to transition customers from VHS to DVD, the format that had completely taken over the business. Can it get any more basic than that? Blockbuster would continue to blame their problems on anything and everything, but the fact is, they never rebuilt their store inventories in DVD and thus never had a chance to succeed as VHS faded away.

How could this happen? It was equivalent to a music store of the day deciding it was not going to stock CDs when that format replaced cassette tapes. Or today, it would be like Best Buy not stocking iPhones in favor of flip phones, or a drug store not stocking multi-blade razors in favor of the single blade version from the 1960s. Yet, that is exactly what Blockbuster did.

By this time, sales at Blockbuster were beginning to falter. Same-store rental revenue declined in 2004 by -6.4 percent, its largest in history. In contrast, we were aggressively transitioning our stores in Alaska and Texas from VHS to DVD. Sales were continuing to grow, and profit was higher than ever. But Blockbuster was going into a decline from which it would never recover. That is why I did the research and discovered their shockingly inadequate inventory. Because of Blockbuster's equally inadequate information systems, these numbers were difficult to decipher. But they are accurate. Blockbuster never disputed them. The problem was obvious, and if not corrected, the decline would only get worse.

I presented the numbers to Blockbuster in ABF board meetings and in documented memos to Blockbuster executives, including John Antioco, Nigel Travis, and Nick Shepherd. Blockbuster's response was shocking. "The customer is *format agnostic*," they told me. Their official position was customers did not care if Blockbuster stocked a title in DVD or VHS. All they wanted was the title. They showed me stacks of research they claimed backed up their position. But by now, 80 million American households had a DVD player, and the average price for one was still about $200. Regardless of Blockbuster's "research," why did so many invest in DVD players if they did not prefer it over VHS? It was a simple question that had a simple answer. Yet, they never wavered.

So, if you visited a Blockbuster store in 2004 and walked the aisles in search of something other than a new release, you would see VHS movies alongside DVD movies. A VHS copy of *The Godfather* may have caught your eye, but the DVD version was missing. That was by design. Blockbuster thought you would just as soon rent the VHS version.

By 2006, VHS was dead, and it was completely removed from the stores. That left Blockbuster with store inventories completely inadequate to profitably move forward. They needed to spend about $50,000 per store, rebuilding the company's inventory, and they had the money to do it at the time. But Blockbuster never fully committed to DVD, and the stores became shells of their former selves. Yet Blockbuster never acknowledged it, and Wall Street did not understand the business well enough to notice.

Then came the issue of the price to rent DVDs at Blockbuster stores. All rental businesses must have an attractive value proposition. People *rent* because it costs less to *buy* the same thing. Because of its low price and wide availability, DVD made the value proposition for video rental stores more important than ever.

DVDs were for sale just about everywhere, and the top new releases could be found at most mass merchants and supermarkets for $15 to $20. These stores usually sold them at or below cost, using them as loss-leaders to help drive customers to stores. In addition, DVD had become such a goldmine for the studios they dug deep into their catalog and dumped thousands of titles on the market at extraordinarily low prices. Every Walmart of the day had huge dump bins all over the store, chocked full of DVDs by the thousands, and priced $3 to $5, about the same price to *rent* the same movies at Blockbuster.

Put simply, the price to *buy* a movie was the *lowest* in history. Yet, the price to *rent* a movie at Blockbuster was the *highest* in history. It gets worse.

John Antioco proudly wore the label of someone who had "defied the status quo" when he brought revenue sharing to Blockbuster. The need for revenue sharing was always attributed to the $65 price for most newly released movies. Stores had to rent them about 20 times just to break even. With DVD, the wholesale cost of almost every new release was about $17. It was a revolution-ary improvement to the video rental business model. Now, a store could buy all the movies it wanted and only had to rent them about four times to break even. And if that was not enough, when rental demand was exhausted, most previously-viewed DVD movies could be sold for at least $8, which netted the actual cost of most DVDs down to about $9. The opportunity to make happier customers with more movies—and make more money doing it—was extraordinary. And although the studios' drive to sell more movies had flatlined rental growth, it was *still* a $10 billion industry—about the same as when DVD was introduced. The opportunities to use lower-cost DVDs to strengthen Block-buster's business were enormous and, for a brief period, that is what they did.

As DVD steadily marched to dominance at the turn of the cen-tury, Blockbuster benefitted tremendously from the dramatically lower wholesale cost of DVD new releases (rental product was by far its largest expense). The higher cost of revenue sharing VHS movies had driven its rental gross margin to as low as 64 percent, the lowest in the history of the company. But as DVD became the dominant format, Antioco chose to shun revenue sharing in favor of its $17 wholesale price, and Blockbuster's rental gross margin skyrocketed to 72 percent, the *highest* in the history of the company. The margin improvement alone generated over $350 million in annual incremental cash flow, a giant windfall of cash gifted by the studios. Blockbuster had done nothing to earn it other than simply buy DVDs for $17, and over the next few years, improved profit margins allowed Blockbuster to retire most of the $1 billion plus of debt incurred from its spin-off from Viacom.

Then inexplicably, in 2003, Antioco took Blockbuster back to revenue sharing. Even with the benefit of almost 20 years of hindsight, there is still no reasonable explanation for why he made the decision to hand control back to the studios and immediately increase its cost to buy DVDs. Blockbuster even stated as much in its 2002 Annual Report: *"The lower sell-through pricing for DVD product has enabled us to acquire significant quantities of product with or without revenue sharing."* But in direct contradiction to this statement, the company was already moving back to revenue sharing in early 2003. Just two years after recording the highest rental gross margin in its history and the dramatic profit increase that came with it, Blockbuster was right back where it was before low-cost DVD took the market by storm. The price for its largest expense, rental product, had been cut by over 50 percent. Yet, shockingly, Blockbuster was spending more for it than ever!

But it was even worse. The video rental market had been mature for several years, and although DVD's low-price appeal to buyers had not killed it, it did minimize the potential for any significant growth. Yet Blockbuster had continued to methodically open *even more* stores. By now, it had over 8,000 and billions in additional operating expenses, fixed costs, and lease liabilities. It had over $2.5 billion in noncancellable lease liabilities alone. If the future of home entertainment would eventually be through electronic delivery of movies, why had Blockbuster so relentlessly added to its brick-and-mortar store base with the billions in fixed costs and liabilities that came with it? Because, as had always been the case, it did not know how to do anything else.

Blockbuster had laid the foundation for certain failure. Although still extremely profitable because of the last bit of windfall profits from $17 DVDs, its reckless mismanagement of the transition to the popular new format had created an untenable situation. Sales trends had turned decisively negative, and Antioco had no answers. When there did not appear to be any way out of the predicament it had created for itself, Blockbuster played the "victim card" and invited all franchisees to join in its pity party.

In April 2004, the ABF held its annual spring meeting, and everyone knew by then that Blockbuster had big problems. And since most franchisees had followed them every step of the way, they had big problems, too, and were desperately looking for answers. It fell upon Nick Shepherd, President of U.S. Store Operations, to rally the troops. The opening slide of his presentation read: "What's really happening to our business, and who's trying to eat our lunch?" His answers to that question were:

> "Consumers are spending more on buying movies at the expense of renting."

"New DVD rentals have not replaced lost VHS rentals."

"The price gap between buying and renting has narrowed too much."

"The Blockbuster brand has weakened due to increased attention to buying."

The list of answers reads like an indictment of everything Blockbuster had done wrong as DVD took over the business, but there was no acknowledgment of how they had created their own problems. How the price to *rent* movies at Blockbuster was the highest in its history, even though the price to *buy* them at Walmart was the lowest in history. Or how its catalog inventory was half that of a few years earlier and priced to *rent* for the same it cost to *buy* the same titles at just about any retailer. Instead, Shepherd doubled down and declared:

"Blockbuster is no longer RELEVANT!"

It was a less-than-uplifting message for the franchisees in the room who still owned over 1,000 stores, many of which were struggling to remain profitable. But he was exactly right. Blockbuster *was* no longer relevant—but of its own doing, not others. This message became Blockbuster's new mantra. We heard it over and over. As time passed, Blockbuster's "irrelevance" gave them permission to take foolish chances, to try things that conflicted with the economics of the business. *Every* initiative they launched in the next three years failed—most spectacularly. But they would excuse the results to the chances they had to take—all because Blockbuster was not *relevant*.

Certainly, there were serious challenges, but most of them had been made worse by Blockbuster—not forces beyond its control. The video rental industry was generating about $10 billion in annual sales. It was *still* America's favorite way to watch a movie. Nothing else came close, and Blockbuster was the undisputed king. There would come a day when renting DVDs *would* become irrelevant. But it was *not* in 2004. Instead of rallying the troops at that spring franchise meeting, Shepherd blamed Blockbuster's problems on others—and surrendered.

As Blockbuster's rental business flattened and began to decline, Antioco had to give shareholders something to believe in. So, instead of focusing on the rental business where Blockbuster was the undisputed king, Antioco turned his attention to the sell-through business, of which *Walmart* was the undisputed king. The announcement made for a good headline:

"Blockbuster to Take Its Rightful Share of the $15 Billion Sell-through DVD Business."

The plan was an easy sell for anyone outside of the video rental business. Antioco declared that Blockbuster would increase its share of the sell-through market from 3 percent to 9 percent, which sounded like a reasonable goal. That would equal about $1 billion in new sales and $250 million in profit, which happened to be a similar amount lost when he inexplicably began revenue sharing $17 DVDs. Antioco went on to say that Blockbuster wouldn't have to sell DVDs at cost like Walmart and other retailers because customers wouldn't drive past Blockbuster to save a couple of dollars elsewhere.

But Antioco's claim ignored the facts. It is common knowledge that most people visit Walmart or grocery stores *every* week, and those stores sold DVDs at or below cost. Only the heaviest movie renters, about 25 percent, visited Blockbuster every week. It was not an issue of people driving *past* Blockbuster to buy a DVD at the grocery store. They were *already there*—every week.

I had the benefit of having seen it from both sides. In my years at H-E-B, it was easy to sell movies. We could sell more from one checkout stand than an entire video store could ever hope to. There was simply no way Blockbuster could convert people from buying DVDs during their normal weekly grocery shopping trip to making an *extra* stop at Blockbuster to buy a DVD—and pay *more*. Anyone who took the time to study how and where customers spent their money knew that.

Antioco's headline-grabbing soundbites kept Wall Street at bay for a time, but soon he learned what we had all known for years. Blockbuster could sell a few DVDs to its existing customers, who wanted it right then and were willing to pay a couple of dollars more, but no one was going to make an *extra* trip to Blockbuster to buy a movie and *spend more* for it. The entire idea was preposterous, and Antioco soon learned he could not deliver on his commitment to triple Blockbuster's DVD sales. So, he did what he so often did. Antioco launched another one of his "big ideas."

Antioco used the holiday season of 2002 to show Wall Street that Blockbuster could and would compete with Walmart. He launched a tragically flawed promotion. Here was the deal. For every DVD you buy at Blockbuster, you get a free rental—no limit! In other words, Blockbuster would trade the $3 profit from a *rental* of a DVD for a $3 profit on the *sale* of a DVD. It sounded innocent enough, but there was a problem. If the only customers who took the deal were existing customers who were renting and buying in the store already, Blockbuster was slashing its profit in half. An upside benefit was only possible if thousands and thousands of new customers changed their shopping habits and came to Blockbuster to rent *and* buy. When Blockbuster announced the promotion and implored franchisees to participate, I thought it was astonishingly misguided, and the results could be catastrophic. Unfortunately for Blockbuster, that is exactly what happened.

The promotion generated millions of free rentals for Blockbuster's existing customers, with no corresponding increase in the sales of DVDs to compensate. The business tanked. It was so devastating that just three weeks after the promotion began, Blockbuster was forced to announce it was lowering sales and profit forecasts for not just the fourth quarter but the entire year. On the day of the announcement, the stock lost $1 billion in value—a 32 percent decline. Antioco would only say: "We may have overestimated how fast consumers would pick up on our being in the retail business."[39] The fact is, customers never did get the message and continued buying movies as a part of their weekly shopping trips to the grocery store, the same as they always had. Antioco never came close to delivering on his commitment to triple movie sales at Blockbuster and cost the company millions trying to prove to Wall Street that he could do the impossible.

The financial damage was so significant, Blockbuster launched a fire drill to improve its stature on Wall Street. It laid off staff, cut back marketing, and slashed buys for rental product that had already been booked. The fire drill left permanent scars, but it was mission accomplished. Early 2003 performance improved, and Antioco proudly announced: "We achieved our highest rental margin since the first quarter of 1998, proving our contention that the fourth quarter of 2002 was an anomaly."[40] There was some truth to that. It *was* an anomaly, but one caused by a misguided promotion that was doomed from the start.

Throughout the transition from VHS to DVD, our stores in Alaska and Texas enjoyed consistently higher sales and even better improvement in profits because of DVD's lower cost. It was difficult for me to understand how it could be any other way. The price for rental product, by far our largest cost, had been cut by more than half. DVD had brought millions more customers to the business. And by now, we knew for sure that the studios' attempt to shift most of the business to sell-through had failed. Americans were *still* renting more DVDs than they purchased. How could a business not thrive in that environment?

As DVD replaced VHS in the early 2000s, we bought twice as many new releases as before and still spent much less. Customers were happier, and we made more money. We used a portion of the incremental profit to heavily invest in DVD catalog titles to replace VHS. The more we bought, the more we rented. Within a few years, our DVD catalog inventory was five times larger than a typical Blockbuster store—and renting five times more. In addition, the convenience of DVD created an entirely new category—television shows—which grew to as much as 20 percent of the business in some of our stores. It had hardly existed at all in the days of VHS.

DVD brought the opportunity to create abundance at attractive prices. Our stores stocked *every* title a customer asked for—*all of them*. We called the program "We've Got It, Or We'll Get It!" If we did not have it, we got it if a customer asked for it. The stores were so crammed with movies, we created what we called Blockbuster Gold sections where customers could more easily find all the most popular catalog titles that were new to DVD. It was a time of incredible abundance and incredible growth.

In 2002, we won Blockbuster's President's Award for having the highest same-store sales growth in the company—over 10 percent. Blockbuster was flat that year and trending downward. In fact, their store sales would decline every year thereafter. I had hoped the recognition from the President's Award would create some interest in what we were doing, which was completely different from everything Blockbuster was doing. I repeatedly asked them to study our stores. Let's at least have a discussion. We were getting consistently phenomenal results as compared to theirs. But neither Antioco nor any other executive at Blockbuster ever showed interest in how we grew our store sales every year, while theirs declined. They would often claim some of their analysts were studying it, but we never had a substantive discussion about it. It was yet another instance of, "Not invented here, not interested." That had been a common theme since Blockbuster's founding, and it never ended.

It so happened that right in the middle of the transition to DVD, I got an opportunity to buy the Blockbuster stores in Alaska and El Paso that I had been running for Prime Cable the past seven years. Prime was in the process of selling all their businesses, the largest of which was their cable television system in Las Vegas. They sold it for $1.325 billion, which, at the time, was one of the largest cable television deals in history. They offered me the first crack to buy their Blockbuster stores. The asking price was $16 million, a small deal for them, but about $16 million more than I had in the bank. What's more, because of Blockbuster's difficulties, bankers considered financing stores extremely risky. Options for both debt and equity were scarce and extremely expensive.

But because of the dramatically improved economics that DVD brought to the business, I believed there was huge growth potential, which was the only way the deal could work because of the high cost of capital. I financed the purchase of the stores with a $13 million loan at 9.75 percent interest and $3 million in cash from a private equity firm that required a 30 percent return on their investment. People would look at that deal and think I was crazy, but that is how much I believed in the benefits DVD brought to the business, and why I could never understand why Blockbuster did not see the same potential.

We closed the purchase in February 2000 and chose the name "Border Entertainment" for our new company because of its proximity to both the southern and northern borders of the United States. Our stores were spread from Fairbanks, Alaska, to Brownsville, Texas—about 5,000 miles. Even stores within the state of Alaska were as much as 1,500 miles apart, and the Texas stores were over 800 miles apart. But we built teams of professional, independent-minded managers who ran the business like it was their own. One could say we were geographically challenged, but it made us stronger because everyone had to successfully play their own distinct role. We could not afford any weak links.

The private equity group exited just four years after we closed the deal with a 40 percent return on their investment, and we retired our loan in 2012, two years *after* Blockbuster filed bankruptcy. We did indeed grow the business and almost tripled the company's profits over the next seven years, the very same years in which Blockbuster's financial results crashed.

Ironically, we bought our stores about the same time Blockbuster went public when it spun off from Viacom. But in sharp contrast to our results, its shareholders lost everything, and its lenders and other creditors got pennies on the dollar when the company filed bankruptcy ten years later. How and why did Blockbuster make the business so hard—so much harder than it needed to be? But it would only get harder. Netflix by-mail was just getting started.

CHAPTER 8

THE NETFLIX YOU DO NOT REMEMBER

"In today's Long Tail markets, the main effect of filters is to help people move from the world they know ('Hits') to the world they don't ('Niches')."

—CHRIS ANDERSON, *THE LONG TAIL*, 2006[41]

When Reed Hastings and Marc Randolph founded Netflix in 1997, Blockbuster was the undisputed king of home entertainment. Netflix was a small company with a passion for being the best. Blockbuster's only passion was being big. Thirteen years later, Blockbuster filed bankruptcy, and Netflix was not just on its way to transforming the *home* entertainment industry, but the *entire* entertainment industry. Today, it is the most valuable entertainment company in the world.

The fate of the two companies was starkly different, as was its leadership. In its 25-year history, Blockbuster had five CEOs, none of whom had much interest in the inner workings of the video rental business. Netflix is still run by its Co-founder, Reed Hastings, who wrote a $1.9 million check 23 years ago to start the company. He is a self-described "math wonk," and it shows in the company's obsession with following the numbers to what its customers want. Blockbuster had thousands of times more data about movie watching than Netflix but rarely used it in productive ways. Even though Netflix was a fraction of the size, its obsession with data created a *knowledge* advantage that became its ultimate weapon against Blockbuster.

In its earliest days, Netflix offered DVDs to rent and sell on its website. It was essentially an extension of a video store to the internet. Netflix rented DVDs one at a time, just like Blockbuster— including late fees. But that was not the edition of Netflix that killed Blockbuster. Had it not been for what happened next, Netflix would have probably failed, and the world would be a very different place.

As Netflix Co-founder Marc Randolph described the epiphany: "Why are we storing all these DVDs in the warehouse? Maybe we could figure out a way to let our customers store the discs. At their houses. On their shelves. Just keep the DVDs as long as they wanted."[42] So, instead of renting DVDs one at a time with due dates and late fees, Netflix changed the game. Three DVDs were shipped to customers, who could keep them as long as they wanted. When returned, Netflix would ship replacements. Customers got all this for a monthly fee—a *subscription* fee. Today, just about anything can be purchased on some type of subscription service, and it started with Randolph's idea to use customers' homes as a warehouse for its DVDs. Netflix subscribers would always have DVDs in their homes to watch. But would subscribers be willing to pay enough for it to work? We know the answer to that.

Netflix's subscription service was a runaway success, and they needed more capital to keep pace with the growth. But it was 2000, the year the dot.com bubble burst and the stock market crashed. Capital markets froze, and even though Netflix had already raised over $100 million from investors, it was running out of money. So, in what is the strangest twist of fate in this entire story, Netflix tried to sell itself to Blockbuster. It was reminiscent of 1986 when Blockbuster founder David Cook ran out of money, and Wayne Huizenga provided the lifeline to keep the company growing. This time, Blockbuster could have been the lifeline for what is now the most valuable entertainment company in the world. But we know that did not happen.

Co-founders Reed Hastings and Marc Randolph, and CFO Barry McCarthy met with John Antioco and his team at Blockbuster's Dallas headquarters in September 2000. The proposal was straightforward. Blockbuster would pay $50 million for Netflix, a relatively small amount of money for Blockbuster, which, at the time, was paying studios over $1.5 billion every year for movies.

As Randolph describes that meeting, Reed Hastings was not only looking for money. He wanted to "join forces." "We will run the online part of the combined business. You will focus on the stores. We will find the synergies that come from the combination, and it will truly be a case of the whole being greater than the sum of its parts."[43] It is not clear what the ownership structure would have been, but Blockbuster had all the leverage and no doubt could have emerged as the majority owner of Netflix.

"Monday morning quarterbacking" can be opportunistic, and nobody, including Hastings, could have predicted the runaway success of Netflix. But in September 2000, DVD was still in its infancy, and Netflix already had 250,000 subscribers. If Netflix just kept up with the growth of DVD players, one could easily see Netflix growing to several million subscribers in a few years. Plus, Hastings had made clear that Netflix's eventual goal was to stream movies on the internet. DVD by mail was the bridge to get there. That's why they named the company *Net*flix.com, not DVDbymail.com.

Reed Hastings wasn't a novice entrepreneur begging for money. He had already founded a successful technology company called Pure Software and sold it for $750 million. He had founded Netflix with his own money and used his credibility to attract another $100 million from outside investors. And now, he wanted to join forces with Blockbuster and help transform it into a modern brand.

But Antioco did not see the potential and rejected the deal outright, explaining to Hastings and his team that their business model was unsustainable. Randolph even detected that Antioco was struggling not to laugh at the proposal.[44] For the next few years, Antioco repeatedly minimized the threat posed by Netflix. He called it a niche business that would never have more than 3 million subscribers, a trivial amount he believed not worthy of his attention. But 3 million Netflix subscribers was equivalent to the active membership of 750 Blockbuster stores, which every year generated far more cash than Hastings' $50 million asking price.

Simple math says the offer should have been seriously considered, but Antioco quickly dismissed it.

With nowhere else to turn for capital, Hastings and his team left that Blockbuster meeting dejected but determined to succeed. They believed they had created something special and resolved, in Randolph's words, to, "Kick [Blockbuster's] ass."[45] They returned to their headquarters, laid off 30 percent of their workforce, and continued to grow the company on a shoestring budget. Just two years later, Netflix was valued at $300 million when it went public and raised $82.5 million in new capital.

When John Antioco left Blockbuster five years later in 2007, Netflix stock was valued at $2 billion (more than Blockbuster), and it was *mailing* DVDs to over 7 million subscribers, equivalent to the active membership of 2,000 Blockbuster stores. *And Netflix had not yet streamed a movie.*

When Blockbuster began in the late 1980s, the runway for growth was wide open. Americans were discovering the freedom of watching movies at home on their own schedule, and the competition was fragmented and undercapitalized. All Blockbuster had to do was open stores faster than everyone else, and they were exceptionally good at it. By opening 3,000 stores in just a few years, they became the biggest force in a brand-new industry.

The competitive arena Netflix entered was completely different. In 1997, the video rental business was mature, with little potential for growth. To build a business, it would have to take customers from already entrenched companies like Blockbuster. The idea of DVDs showing up in your mailbox had some appeal, but it also had many inherent inefficiencies. It would be impossible for Netflix to compete with video stores on new releases because those DVDs would spend too much idle time in shipping and processing. As Co-Founder Marc Randolph explained: "To keep our customers happy and our costs reasonable, we needed to direct users to less in-demand movies that we knew they'd like—and probably like even better than new releases."[46]

Netflix could succeed only if it kept customers happy by renting mostly older movies—the catalog. They couldn't have known at the time, but they were attacking Blockbuster's Achilles' heel. Blockbuster had never paid much attention to its catalog movies and had built a business that was almost totally dependent on new releases. They did not even have an efficient management information system to track their catalog movies. They paid little attention to it, and the results showed. Most of those catalog movies were dust collectors on store shelves.

To make matters exponentially worse, Blockbuster had not rebuilt its catalog inventory in DVD, relying for years on worn-out copies of VHS to compete with the newer DVDs Netflix was mailing its subscribers. The fact is, Netflix built an entire business renting primarily older movies, most of which Blockbuster did not stock and all of which were horribly overpriced. Netflix subscribers paid about $20 a month to rent an average of eight DVDs. Those same eight DVDs at Blockbuster, if they had them, would cost at least $32, plus late fees, gas, and time.

In the end, about 80 percent of the DVDs Netflix mailed to its subscribers were older movies—the catalog. Because of Blockbuster's deficient management information systems, it was impossible to know exactly how many catalog titles Blockbuster rented, but it was somewhere around 10 percent. The other 90 percent was new releases. Netflix had built a business Blockbuster couldn't relate to and never understood.

If Blockbuster customers rented mostly new releases, how did Netflix win them over by renting primarily older movies? The answer to that most clearly defines what Netflix was and what Blockbuster was not. Millions of renters walked through Blockbuster stores every week, but most walked straight to the walls of new releases. Catalog movies covered most of the sales floor, yet most customers ignored them because of poor selection and high prices. In contrast, Netflix's only merchandising tool was a subscriber's computer screen (iPhones had not been invented yet). How did they so effectively suggest older movies subscribers would love?

The answer is they became obsessed with understanding what subscribers watched and why. Netflix understood that there were thousands of movies as good or better than the new releases of the day. But that did not matter unless subscribers believed the same.

To address this challenge, Netflix built elaborate algorithms to suggest older titles to its customers. Over time, these algorithms got better and better. But never satisfied, Netflix conducted a very public contest that awarded a $1 million prize to anyone who could improve on their recommendation model (called Cinematch) by 10 percent. As an example of how far Netflix had come, it took three years for someone to improve what it had already built, and Netflix awarded the $1 million prize to a group from AT&T that finally did it.

Even though Blockbuster had a massive database more than fifteen years in the making, Netflix proved it better understood movie renters than Blockbuster ever had or ever would. And they built a massive base of loyal customers by renting movies that Blockbuster did not think their customers cared about.

Netflix had successfully tapped into what was becoming a generational shift, which Chris Anderson described in his ground-breaking book *The Long Tail: Why the Future of Business is Selling Less of More*. It was published in 2006 and describes how the world was being transformed by the internet and the near limitless choice it provides consumers. Anderson describes the declining impact of "the hits" as customers discovered the "long tail" titles via the internet. Blockbuster never recognized this trend, and Netflix opportunistically filled the vacuum.

Blockbuster should have been at the forefront of the "long tail" phenomenon because it had the data to understand it better than anyone. Millions of customers streamed through Blockbuster stores every week. But instead of capitalizing on their expanding interests in older movies, Blockbuster did the opposite—they stocked fewer of them and overpriced the ones they had. Blockbuster was content to pursue a business model that was dependent on hits, but as *The Long Tail* so effectively explains, that was quickly becoming a thing of the past. Netflix was blazing a trail to the future.

Netflix so effectively matched movies to the tastes of its subscribers, it kept them happy, although it rarely mailed the titles they wanted to see the most. Subscribers used a queue system to list the movies they wanted to watch in the order of preference. In a perfect world, subscribers would receive the title at the top of their queue, followed by number 2, number 3, and so on. But that rarely happened. Netflix had the "right to choose" and used this system to control its cost of product and support its guarantee of overnight delivery to most subscribers.

The queue system is especially important to this story because a Blockbuster store could not duplicate it. In a video store, the *customer* always had the "right to choose." This would play a critical role as Blockbuster tried to answer Netflix's by-mail subscription service with an "in-store" version. As would be the case in virtually all of Blockbuster's attempts to answer the Netflix challenge, it tried to play by Netflix's rules instead of capitalizing on its own strengths. This led to critical errors that ultimately doomed Blockbuster.

In contrast, Netflix understood its weaknesses and created effective alternatives. It built on its strengths and minimized its weaknesses. Blockbuster did the exact opposite. When it finally acknowledged Netflix as a threat, Blockbuster repeatedly minimized the strengths of its stores and enhanced their weaknesses. It started with Blockbuster's in-store version of a subscription service that was meant to mirror Netflix, which, of course, was impossible.

By 2004, four years after Netflix's failed attempt to partner with Blockbuster, it had grown its subscribers from 250,000 to over 2 million—equivalent to about 500 Blockbuster stores. And the pace of growth was accelerating. Netflix projected over 4 million subscribers by 2005. At Blockbuster headquarters in Dallas, panic was beginning to set in. Same-store rental revenue had been flat to negative for four years, and the decline was accelerating. In 2004, Blockbuster would register the worst U.S. same-store rental revenue decline in its now almost 20-year history. Antioco summed up the situation: "I used to think it [Netflix subscribers] was a maximum of 3 million customers, but I think Netflix has shown that it can be higher than that."[47]

As Netflix stole customers during the past five years, there were a number of effective ways that Blockbuster could have responded. Yet, it had done nothing other than minimize Netflix as a threat. There was still time, but Blockbuster's first serious attempt only made Netflix stronger and Blockbuster weaker.

In May 2004, Blockbuster rolled out what it called the Movie Pass. It played well in the press. "The long-awaited national launch of Blockbuster Video's in-store movie subscription program has finally come, making the offer available in all of the chain's more than 5,000 stores in the U.S."[48] It was yet another headline-grabbing announcement from Blockbuster. But it had no chance of succeeding.

The Movie Pass sounded innocent enough on the surface. It was "Netflix-in-a-store." Pay a monthly fee, keep two or three DVDs out at a time. No late fees. But there was a problem. Remember that *Netflix* had the "right to choose" which DVDs customers rented and thus effectively drove subscribers to older movies with its Cinematch recommendation system. At Blockbuster, *Movie Pass subscribers* had the "right to choose." And since Blockbuster was so singularly focused on new releases, that was about all they had to rent. Their catalog inventories were woefully inadequate to support a profitable subscription program. So, as you might guess, Movie Pass subscribers rented primarily new releases. And even though they represented a small minority of Blockbuster's customers, Movie Pass subscribers rented a disproportionately large number of new releases, which left fewer for other customers to rent. The program had weakened Blockbuster's biggest strength in its battle with Netflix: the instant gratification of renting new releases in a store.

Blockbuster acknowledged the dilemma in an ABF board meeting. "We are victims of our own success." Translation: The bigger the Movie Pass got, the worse things got for Blockbuster. There were fewer new releases to rent, which weakened its biggest advantage over Netflix. But that did not stop Blockbuster from pushing franchisees to jump on board and, as was often the case, most franchisees blindly followed their leader. Over 900 of the 1,100 franchise stores chose to sell the Movie Pass, and soon, already weak sales trends became worse.

Our company was one of the few who took a wait-and-see approach. There were too many unanswered questions, the first being: "How many customers are already spending more than the $20 monthly subscription fee?" I may still want to sell the Movie Pass, but I need to know how many customers may trade down. That information was not in our store computer system nor FBOS, the franchise back office management system. Amazingly, Blockbuster couldn't answer that question either!

As sales got worse, franchisees continued to push for answers. How many movies were Movie Pass subscribers renting? What titles? But Blockbuster dodged the questions. Finally, the ABF board formally requested the information in a letter to Blockbuster executives, and, at long last, they answered the question. By this time, the answer shouldn't have come as a surprise. They did not know. Their response read:

"Currently the POS [store computer system] does not break down this information for reporting purposes. To enable the POS to break down reporting at this level would require significant investment in re-coding. There are currently no plans to make this required investment."

And they never did. Blockbuster acknowledged that some customers were trading down, but they never knew how many. Later, they began to provide anecdotal "snapshot" data, but it was not available on a store-by-store basis or in any level of detail. Franchisees never knew exactly what DVDs Movie Pass subscribers were renting, and we had no reason to believe Blockbuster did either.

Netflix was passionate about understanding what all their subscribers were renting, and they used this data to create intensely loyal customers. In stark contrast, Blockbuster's first response to Netflix did not have a reporting system that could show franchisees what Movie Pass customers were renting and, as a result, they couldn't understand its effect on sales or rental behavior. As was the case with so many Blockbuster initiatives, they were running in the blind.

To outside observers, the Movie Pass made it appear like Blockbuster had answered Netflix's challenge. Many on Wall Street believed Netflix's days were numbered. How could a still relatively small company take on mighty Blockbuster and win? But Blockbuster was in a weakened condition, and it was getting worse by the day. Their stores did not have sufficient inventory to compete with Netflix, and the Movie Pass had only made it worse. Store sales continued to plummet, and there was no end in sight. Throughout the organization, a belief began to set in that Blockbuster stores were in permanent decline. There was no discussion about what they had done to make it worse, only that they had done everything they could, and it was not working.

So in 2004, John Antioco made what appeared to be the obvious decision. Blockbuster would create its own DVD-by-mail service to compete with Netflix. They would take on the fast-growing upstart on their own turf. Surely, *this* would be the beginning of the end for Netflix. When Blockbuster's plans leaked out, Netflix stock dropped 60 percent. The sleeping giant had awakened, and it was just a matter of time before it would take down Netflix. Right?

Wrong.

By now, Netflix had raised hundreds of millions in capital. It had built one of the most advanced websites on the internet that successfully engaged customers and built intense loyalty. Netflix had also built an enviable distribution system that provided overnight delivery to almost all its subscribers. They even had a distribution center in Anchorage, Alaska, that shipped DVDs overnight all over the state in competition with our company's franchised stores. Netflix had been built from the ground up by what was now a highly experienced management team, led by people like CEO Reed Hastings and Chief Content Officer Ted Sarandos, who would become two of the most influential people in the business world.

Blockbuster was ill-prepared to take on Netflix. Even though internet-based businesses were always considered the biggest threat to its dominance of home entertainment, the company had done virtually nothing to build digital competency within the organization. But instead of searching for an experienced executive outside the company to run its new internet business, Antioco stayed inside and chose Shane Evangelist, who jokingly says he got the job because, "I could spell it [internet]."[49] And even though Netflix had already invested hundreds of millions building its business, Evangelist's budget was only $25 million.

When Evangelist joined Blockbuster in 2000, he was 26 years old and had just completed his MBA at Southern Methodist University. Prior to joining Blockbuster, he was a successful business unit executive at IBM for four years and had distinguished himself by selling computer products and services to Blockbuster. He had grown the account from $10 million to over $100 million while at IBM and made a name for himself by helping reengineer the store checkout process.

Evangelist was a born leader. He was captain of his top-ranked gymnastics team at the University of New Mexico, as well as the school's student body president. Blockbuster hired him away from IBM just as he had been promoted to a senior sales position. Although he was young and had no experience in the video rental business, he began his career at Blockbuster as Vice President of Strategic Planning, where he led a task force to develop alternative sources of revenue for the stores. Out of that project came the previously discussed Radio Shack and Round Table Pizza ventures, both of which failed.

Other than helping streamline the store checkout process while at IBM, Evangelist had no experience in the video rental business, but he quickly became known as "John's boy." He was extremely self-assured and, with the unquestioned backing from Antioco, was referred to by some as the "Shane-train." Evangelist was equally loyal to Antioco, who had placed him in a critical senior-level executive role in a major corporation at the age of 26. He still reveres Antioco and glowingly says he was "always the smartest one in the room" and the smartest CEO Evangelist has ever known. The truth is, Evangelist did not know enough about the video rental business to judge what Antioco did or did not know. As time passed, I began to believe that is exactly the way Antioco wanted it.

Evangelist added a few key people to round out the leadership team, but most of the programming was done by outside consultants. They launched "Blockbuster Online" just six months later in August 2004, which was, no doubt, a remarkable accomplishment. They had built a website and a network of distribution centers across the country. Antioco boasted: "There will be no reason why a customer would choose Netflix over Blockbuster based on price, service, or breadth of selection."[50] That statement was nothing more than a wishful claim with no corresponding action plan. Blockbuster never came close to duplicating Netflix's legendary service or its Cinematch recommendation system. Nor did it fully commit to overnight delivery, which was a critical component of Netflix's success.

Unable to match Netflix's service, Blockbuster started a price war. It also offered subscribers two free in-store rentals per month, which on top of the excess demand already created by the Movie Pass, made the availability of new releases even worse, and the weak sales trends persisted. Antioco claimed Blockbuster's by-mail business would break even at 2 million subscribers, which it hoped to reach by the end of 2005, about 16 months after launch. By using lower prices, free rentals, and its still powerful brand, Blockbuster Online attracted a half-million subscribers a few months after launch. At the time, that was one of the fastest ramp-ups of any website in history. But growth soon stalled, and the goal of 2 million subscribers was nowhere in sight.

Struggling to regain momentum, Blockbuster ran a commercial during the 2005 Super Bowl that mocked its own stores. It showed a husband telling his wife he was going to Blockbuster to rent a movie. He backed his car to the end of the driveway, pulled a DVD from the mailbox, and returned to the garage. Blockbuster was using the massive viewing audience of the Super Bowl to highlight the inconvenience of driving to its 5,000 U.S. stores! Netflix could not have been more pleased.

The attention generated from the Super Bowl ad produced a brief spike in subscribers, but Blockbuster Online could not compete head-to-head with Netflix, and growth soon slowed. By the end of the year, Blockbuster Online still had only 1.2 million subscribers, a little more than half its goal, and was still very unprofitable.

Although Netflix had 4.2 million subscribers and was growing faster, its financials had taken a hit because of the price war with Blockbuster. As Reed Hastings described it, Blockbuster had thrown everything at them but the kitchen sink, at which point John Antioco had someone go to Home Depot and send him a kitchen sink. It had gotten personal with Antioco, and he seemed to be enjoying the fight.

But more than two years after its launch, Blockbuster Online was a failure. Free in-store rentals and lower subscription prices had failed to slow down Netflix; Blockbuster was losing the war and a lot of money in the process. Desperate times called for desperate measures, so it was time for Antioco to launch another one of his "big ideas." This one would turn Blockbuster Online into a parasite, and the stores were its host.

The new version of Blockbuster Online was called "Total Access." There is an old business adage that mocks lazy marketing schemes. It goes: "Anybody can give it away!" Total Access took "giving it away" to an entirely new level—an absurd level. It launched in November 2006, and the offering was simple. Now, Blockbuster Online subscribers had the option to return DVDs through the mail as usual *or* return them to a Blockbuster store where they could immediately rent another DVD—*for free*. Most of these free movies were new releases, and there was no limit to how many times subscribers could repeat the process. They could do it every day if they chose!

People love "free stuff," so, not surprisingly, growth accelerated. Total Access attracted 750,000 new subscribers in just six weeks, and the 2 million subscriber goal was finally reached. And for the first time ever, Blockbuster was signing up more new subscribers than Netflix. Blockbuster had done what Netflix could not because it had no stores. Now, Total Access subscribers could get the instant gratification of going to a store to get a movie instead of waiting for delivery through the mail—for free. Blockbuster was celebrating, and much of Wall Street was falling in line; everyone believed that, at long last, Netflix had finally met its match.

Antioco and Evangelist were suddenly basking in adulation as the ones who finally slowed down the Netflix juggernaut. But at what cost? Before the launch of Total Access, the availability of new releases in the stores was already the worst in years because of the Movie Pass. Now, millions more DVDs were being removed by Total Access subscribers—for free. But *every* rental had a cost. Simply put, Blockbuster could not afford to stock enough new releases for its store customers *plus* Total Access subscribers. The transformation of Blockbuster Online into Total Access had created a parasite that was sucking the stores dry. Almost overnight, the availability of new releases was the worst it had *ever* been—even worse than when the old VHS cassette version cost $65 apiece.

Blockbuster claimed Total Access would break even if it reached 5 million subscribers, and that appeared attainable at the time. But it was never clear how that was calculated because it was impossible to quantify the damage being done to the stores due to the dramatic increase in out-of-stocks. It was as if Antioco and Evangelist did not understand the economics of a Blockbuster store. It was impossible to keep the stores adequately stocked when the Total Access parasite was sucking the life out of them. Sales continued to plummet and, predictably, the cost of product skyrocketed in Blockbuster's failed attempt to buy enough new releases to keep the stores stocked. By the end of 2007, rental revenue had dropped another 7 percent and rental gross margin had fallen to an historical low of 61 percent. Blockbuster's financial difficulties had reached a crisis point. But they were about to be offered a lifeline.

Few knew at the time, but Blockbuster had a way out of the predicament it had created. In January 2007, while both Antioco and Reed Hastings attended the Sundance Film Festival, a meeting was arranged at Hastings' chalet. He had said publicly many times that Total Access was not sustainable; he was more accurate than he knew because of what it was doing to Blockbuster's stores. But Hastings did not know how long before Blockbuster would collapse and was under pressure from shareholders to fight back. So, in a reversal of the scenario from seven years earlier when Netflix tried to sell the company to Blockbuster, Hastings offered to buy Blockbuster's online business. That meeting became a badge of honor for Antioco. He had finally gotten Hastings' attention.

A price was not discussed at the meeting, but a formal offer was subsequently made for $200 per subscriber, which would have equaled about $700 million. Netflix even offered ongoing payments to service in-store exchanges for Blockbuster's Total Access subscribers, which could have added hundreds of millions more to the price. The offer was formally discussed at a meeting of Blockbuster's board of directors in early 2007. Led by Shane Evangelist, Blockbuster management recommended the board not accept the offer. Evangelist believed Blockbuster had all the momentum, and if Netflix would pay $700 million now, they would pay a lot more later. The board agreed, and the offer was rejected.

Antioco could have saved Blockbuster right then. He could have fully retired its debt, rebuilt the stores' depleted inventory, and returned the company to profitability. Blockbuster would have been well-positioned to make the transition to movie delivery via the internet, which is where everyone knew the business was going. But Antioco wouldn't be around to explain why he had not taken the offer. Soon afterward, he announced his resignation.

While we watched Blockbuster's stores crumble at the hands of Netflix, our franchise stores in Alaska and Texas were stronger than ever. In 2007, the year Antioco left Blockbuster, we enjoyed our most profitable year ever and were still growing. Was there something unique about our markets that allowed us to thrive while Blockbuster's stores were dying? The opposite was true. Netflix was particularly appealing to Alaskans because so many traveled great distances on icy roads to our stores. DVDs delivered by mail were especially appealing. Yet our Alaska stores were the most profitable in the entire Blockbuster system, and our Texas stores were more profitable than ever. How did that happen?

The answer was simple. We built on the *strengths* of our Blockbuster stores instead of weakening them by trying to be "*Netflix*-in-a-store." We exploited Netflix's weaknesses. We took advantage of low-priced DVDs to buy more than twice as many new releases than ever before. With its inherent inefficiencies of sending those same movies through the mail, Netflix could not compete. Blockbuster did the opposite. By making its stores the host for the parasite that was Total Access, its availability of new releases was the worst in its history. It had eliminated its biggest advantage.

Netflix's biggest strength was its huge selection of "long tail" product. They stocked virtually every DVD available, but because Netflix had the "right to choose," its massive selection was not always available to subscribers. They, in fact, punished heavy users by sending them mostly titles at the end of their queue, which came to be known as "throttling." It was a significant weakness Blockbuster could have exploited but never did.

In our stores, we dramatically increased our DVD catalog inventory and lowered prices. Blockbuster did the opposite. They reduced inventory and raised prices. Our stores did not have every DVD like Netflix, but we did have *every* DVD each store's customers had requested, which effectively built an inventory customized to each store's customer base. And, perhaps most importantly, our *customers* got to choose what to rent, not Netflix. There was no *throttling* in our Blockbuster stores.

Visiting our Blockbuster stores was more exciting than ever. They were loaded with new releases that could take weeks for Netflix subscribers to receive and stocked with every catalog title customers had ever requested. Plus, instead of being guided by Netflix.com to the titles *they* wanted you to watch, our customers roamed freely through the stores, choosing from thousands of titles they could hold in their hands while visiting with other customers and helpful employees along the way. While some did prefer DVDs by mail, the experience of visiting our stores was clearly winning the day. We had more customers than ever before, and profit had increased 250 percent since Netflix came on the scene.

Throughout those years, I used ABF board meetings with Blockbuster executives to discuss how we were thriving, even as Netflix was growing. I showed them our results and how we did it. I contrasted our inventories and pricing schemes with theirs to point out obvious weaknesses. When I got only polite disagreement in meetings, I sent detailed memos to John Antioco, Nigel Travis, Nick Shepherd, and others. They rarely answered and, when they did, it was always limited to polite "corporate-speak." They never followed up in any meaningful way, and I eventually stopped trying because it was a waste of my time.

There is no reason to believe Blockbuster could not have run successful stores for several more years, the same as we did in Alaska and Texas. Just as Netflix used its DVD-by-mail business to build a bridge to streaming on the internet, Blockbuster could have done the same with its stores. Even though Netflix was the darling of Wall Street and was grabbing most of the headlines, at least five times more people still preferred to rent DVDs in stores instead of by mail. But John Antioco consistently made decisions that weakened Blockbuster stores in what seemed to be a personal fight with Reed Hastings and Netflix.

None of this is to say that Blockbuster should or should not have built a by-mail DVD service to challenge Netflix directly. An argument can be made for both. But what it could not do is destroy the stores in the process. That was never an option because of the billions in fixed costs and other liabilities that had to be paid. The stores were Blockbuster's only source of profit. Yet Blockbuster destroyed them, trying to turn them into Netflix—which was, of course, impossible.

CHAPTER 9

IT'S OVER

"They are under such pressure...they felt they had to try something. What they think of as creative, the rest of us think of as desperate."

—REED HASTINGS, NETFLIX CHAIRMAN AND CEO

It was December 2004. We were in the Blockbuster executive conference room in Dallas. It was the latest in a series of special ABF board meetings meant to keep us apprised of John Antioco's next "big idea." He planned to eliminate late fees. Everyone outside his closest circle of associates thought he was crazy. The ABF board had formally objected to the plan, but our concerns had been mostly ignored. Antioco never attended ABF board meetings, but he attended this one to solicit our support. He knew we did not believe in his latest "big idea" and had come to tell us *we* were the ones who were crazy.

For years, Antioco had disassociated himself from franchisees, so his title was his only source of credibility. He was still the Chairman and CEO, so we gave him his due and listened as he confirmed that Blockbuster would indeed eliminate late fees in a few weeks. He condescendingly shot down anyone who questioned his plan, including me. He reminded us of how Blockbuster had been rendered irrelevant because of Netflix's relentless attack on late fees. He acknowledged he was putting the financial viability of the company at risk but told us he had no choice.

Many have asked: didn't Blockbuster *have* to eliminate late fees? People hated them. But would the same be said of a rental car company, or an equipment rental company, or a wedding supply rental company? Any company that rents things? Would the product you reserved to rent be waiting for you if the rental company did not know when the previous renter was returning it?

As I write this, the COVID-19 virus has disrupted supply chains. The evidence is everywhere, but most notably in grocery stores where toilet paper and hundreds of other staple products are in short supply. It is a startlingly clear example of how sensitive supply chains can be. They are built to meet expected demand, and when that falls out of balance, supply chains break down.

The supply chain at Blockbuster stores was extremely fragile for the following reason. When customers rented DVDs in Blockbuster stores, *they* became an integral part of the supply chain. If customers did not return DVDs on time, supply no longer met demand, and the supply chain broke down. That is why late fees were charged— to keep the supply chain intact. The fact is most customers *did* return DVDs on time and never paid late fees. A minority did not, but there were enough of them to break the supply chain if late fees were not charged to encourage the timely return of DVDs.

Antioco's decision to end late fees was his most glaring example yet of throwing a reckless "big idea" at a problem that had been made worse by years of mismanagement. Blockbuster pursued late fees more aggressively than any other chain. It began with their accounting system, which accrued late fees to revenue as they *occurred*, not when they were *collected* (every other video store company only recorded late fees when they were collected). Uncollected late fees were charged to a budgeted expense line called "bad debt," and if store managers did not control it, they could lose their job. This established a contentious relationship between stores and customers that could have been eliminated but never was.

Blockbuster was the only chain that sent invoices to customers for late fees, even if the DVDs rented had been returned. It was like an irritating invitation not to come back. They also experimented with various return dates and times, but most were meant to *increase* late fee revenue, not make late fees more tolerable for customers. There were a number of ways to reduce the negative connotation of late fees. Eliminating them was never a viable option, but Antioco did it anyway. Ending late fees broke down the supply chain and was the beginning of the end for Blockbuster. It was and still is the most reckless business decision I have ever witnessed.

Antioco had teased the idea in a memo almost a year earlier. "Beginning this month, we will conduct corporate tests to improve our domestic rental proposition, specifically in regards to the elimination of customer resentment associated with EVFs [Late Fees]. We are also aware that some of our franchisees have been conducting their own tests..." He did not identify the franchisees, but we knew who it was. And it was not *some*. It was *one*, Mitch Kerns, a relative newcomer, having opened his first Blockbuster franchise store in the small town of Ottumwa, Iowa, in 2000. He had since opened more and acquired others for a total of eight. They were scattered in small towns in Iowa and California, as well as two in Lake Tahoe.

Kerns had some uniquely competitive situations and was experimenting with what he referred to as the "Buddy Club." It was essentially an appeal to customers to be a buddy to other customers. If enough of them returned movies on time, he would not charge late fees to anyone. He set up an elaborate phone call system to encourage customers to return movies on time. The day a movie was late, the customer was called. He had essentially replaced late fees with a phone call system that kept the supply chain intact. As a result, most customers returned movies on time, and the program was a success.

Kerns had kept the ABF board informed of what he was doing. He cautioned that although the program worked for him, he believed his situation was unique, and anyone trying it should proceed with caution. For various reasons, no other franchisees attempted his plan. But when Antioco learned of Kerns' program, he set up a lunch meeting to learn more. Kerns explained it as described above. The program can only work if most customers bring the movies back, and that was dependent on an aggressive phone call system to encourage a timely return.

Soon after his meeting with Kerns, Antioco directed Nick Shepherd to test his own version of the elimination of late fees. The test was launched in early 2004 in Chattanooga, Tennessee, a city of about 300,000 in the foothills of the Smoky Mountains. Soon afterward, Shepherd began reporting positive results in ABF Board meetings. Knowing of Kerns' program, we were skeptical and had a lot of questions. How much did it cost? How long were customers keeping movies if there were no due dates and no late fees? What were in-stock conditions? What happened to rental revenue, the lifeblood of the business? And finally, was a phone call system used to keep the supply chain intact?

Blockbuster was short on details. The fact is, they never provided detailed answers to most of the questions asked by the ABF board. Most importantly, they never told us exactly what happened to rental revenue without late fees. When we pushed back, Shepherd vehemently defended the plan and pointed to research he believed proved that late fees were killing Blockbuster and had to be eliminated. It was as if the Chattanooga test did not matter. The decision had been made, and nothing was going to stop them.

With no late fees to control the supply chain, it was understood that customers would keep new releases longer, and stores would need more DVDs to stay in stock. Blockbuster's national rollout plan included a 3 percent increase in new release purchases, or $105 million. Yet, when pressed, they acknowledged that they had bought closer to 20 percent more in the Chattanooga test— almost seven times more. Had Blockbuster done that in the national rollout, it would have cost at least $600 million, money they did not have.

The television commercial to announce the end of late fees included music from Roy Orbison's classic song "It's Over." Years later, Antioco joked that when he first saw the commercial, he wondered if *late fees* were "over"—or his *career*[51]. He knew how risky it was—the riskiest decision Antioco ever made. Late fees generated over $300 million in sales, which fell directly to the bottom line. At the time, $300 million was roughly equivalent to the company's entire profit, but Antioco believed the program would attract so many new customers it would reduce overall profit by only $33 million.

At best, the Chattanooga test was inconclusive. But even if the results had been unquestionably positive, should Blockbuster have risked the entire company on a twelve-store test in a southeastern city of 300,000 people? Was that a viable sample for a company with 5,000 stores serving markets of 300 million? Blockbuster did launch one more test in Fresno, California, in September 2004, but results came too late to factor in the decision. Ultimately, Blockbuster eliminated late fees based on *one* test and provided franchisees no conclusive data to show its impact on profit. Antioco's end-of-late-fees scheme was nothing more than a foolhardy roll of the dice.

At the time, our company had 28 stores that served markets with a combined population of about 1.5 million—five times the size of Chattanooga. By any standard, we had been the best-performing stores in the Blockbuster system for several years. Measured by sales trends, profit, market share, anything—we had the best record. No franchise group or corporate store group came close. Desperate to stop Blockbuster from destroying itself, I wrote multiple memos to Antioco and other executives pleading that other options be considered. I reviewed our results in detail and how we achieved them. It was a last-ditch effort to get them to reconsider. But not surprisingly, none of those memos were ever answered.

Nothing would stop Antioco's end-of-late-fees juggernaut. To justify the decision, Blockbuster provided franchisees a draft of the presentation it used to sell the plan to its board of directors. The presentation was full of "corporate speak" to sway board members who had only a cursory understanding of the business. It contained charts, graphs, and consumer research that cast Blockbuster as a victim of forces out of its control, how it had lost "relevance," and described a desperate company that had to make a "bold" move to reverse its fortunes.

The presentation provided a long list of reasons why the company was so desperate, but nothing about what it did to cause its own problems. It pointed out how Blockbuster's "value for the money" had declined but did not mention they had raised rental prices by *over 50 percent* the past few years. In fact, in direct contradiction with its own logic, it included a plan to raise prices even more. It listed what customers liked most about renting: at the top was "finding something I have not seen before," yet the presentation did not mention how its catalog inventory was less than half the size of just five years before. Blockbuster did not *have* what most people "had not seen before." The presentation went on to point out customers' "aggravation and frustration" with paying late fees but did not speak to Blockbuster's own collection policies, which were by far the most aggressive in the industry. Finally, it discussed customers' "feelings" about *not* paying late fees, which—to no one's surprise—was positive.

As I would learn doing research for this book, Antioco's *feelings* had played a major role in many decisions throughout his career. He often told people, "You've just got to feel it," while pointing at his stomach, casting himself as one who made bold decisions that defied the status quo. His feelings must have been the determining factor in this case because, by any measure, he did not have the facts to support so risky a decision. He was about to put the financial future of the entire company in jeopardy based on an inconclusive test in a city of 300,000 people.

In that ABF board meeting in December 2004, Antioco presented no new statistics to back up his decision because there were not any. He answered all questions with a condescending glare that clearly meant, "You just don't get it." And he was right. We did not *get it*. And we certainly did not *feel it*.

That meeting was the saddest day of my professional life, and I was close to tears when I left the conference room. There was not a doubt in my mind that John Antioco had just doomed Blockbuster.

Backed by a massive advertising campaign, Blockbuster's end-of-late-fees program launched January 1, 2005. Kerns, the franchisee who seemed to have started it all, was shocked to learn that Blockbuster's version of no late fees bore no resemblance to his. Instead of keeping return dates the same and asking customers to support the change by returning movies on time, Blockbuster essentially lengthened the rental period by a week, which we all knew spelled disaster. And the language used to describe the plan led to customer confusion and legal action. Here is the actual language from the press release that announced the end of late fees.

> Under the "no late fees" program, Blockbuster still has due dates—one week for games and two days or one week for movies. However, if customers need to keep the product an extra day or two, they can, stress-free. Blockbuster now gives customers a one-week grace

period at no additional charge. At that point, if customers want to keep the movie or game longer, they can. Blockbuster will automatically sell them the product, less the rental fee. If customers decide they don't want to own the movie or game, they simply return the product within 30 days for full credit to their account, less a minimal restocking fee.

Simple, right? Customers were totally confused. "You say there are no late fees. But if I keep it more than a week after the due date, you are going to charge me the full price of the DVD—as much as $30. Isn't that a late fee? And even if I decide to return it later, you are going to charge me a restocking fee. Isn't that just another name for a late fee?"

State attorneys general agreed, and 47 states joined forces to sue Blockbuster for deceptive advertising. The case was settled for $630,000 and Blockbuster's pledge to better communicate the program. The bad press generated was certainly much more destructive than the relatively small fine.

Despite the initial confusion, the novelty effect of such a dramatic change drove more traffic to Blockbuster stores. But unlike Kerns' program, there were no phone calls to customers to encourage timely return, and millions kept DVDs long after what Blockbuster continued to call "due dates." Not surprisingly, the supply chain totally collapsed. And right on schedule, out-of-stocks exploded. To see for myself, I visited several corporate Blockbuster stores, and each one was an embarrassment. Bright, shiny stores—with empty new release walls.

By the summer of 2005, the situation had gotten so bad that

Blockbuster tried to "promote" its way out of the problem with a "Guaranteed In-Stock" campaign to convince customers that they *had* what they did not have—new releases. They must have believed if they said it enough, customers would believe it. But the opposite was true. Millions of customers who did not find the title they were looking for received credits for free rentals. The "Guaranteed In-Stock" program served only to highlight the problem—and cost Blockbuster millions of free rentals in the process.

Undeterred, Antioco boasted that the end of late fees was performing exactly as expected. He even claimed to be outperforming the franchisees who refused to go along with him. But all of his comparisons cherry-picked innocuous data that had little to do with sales or profits. His claims were made without consideration of context, were extremely misleading, and—in the case of our stores—totally false. I was so angry I was briefly tempted to go to the local press to defend our stores, to explain how we had outperformed Blockbuster for much of the last 20 years and was not desperate enough to throw a "Hail Mary" that had no chance of succeeding. And, most importantly, how we still had new releases in stock—and they did not. But I knew better and stayed quiet.

Instead, we focused on explaining to our customers why late fees were necessary. If we did not know when movies would be returned, we could not have them for others to rent, and we might have to resort to raising prices to buy more, which was never a good solution. We posted signs in our stores and handed out letters that explained our position. I signed all the letters and included an email address for customers to ask questions or complain. Most importantly, we held store meetings to explain our position and ensure that all employees understood it, complete with answers to all the questions we believed would be asked. Our employees fielded thousands of questions, but not one customer sent me an email to complain. They had no problem with late fees if they were administered fairly. With rare exception, our customers "got it" and seemed to understand our business better than Antioco.

Blockbuster's decision to end late fees was big news in the press, as well as late-night talk shows. And it became a big story in our markets when the local press learned we were not following Blockbuster's lead. I fielded countless calls from reporters wanting to know why we continued to charge late fees. My answer was simple: "It's best for our customers. If we do not know when movies are being returned, we can't have them for other customers." I got no push back from the press. Like our customers, reporters seemed to understand the business better than Blockbuster, too.

The instant my comments to the press reached Blockbuster, I received a call from the Vice President of Franchising. She was close to unhinged in her anger; she claimed I was speaking negatively about Blockbuster, which was prohibited by the Franchise Agreement. I explained that neither our store people nor I had said anything negative about Blockbuster. We simply stated we believed the program was wrong for *our* customers and why. Blockbuster was spending millions of dollars in advertising to tell the country that late fees were bad and a thing of the past. It was a huge challenge to counter the television commercials that were running nonstop. Did we not have the right to tell *our* side of the story to *our* customers? She eventually backed off.

Late fees could be an irritant, but they were a necessary component of running a rental business and keeping the supply chain intact. There were plenty of ways to make them more tolerable without eliminating them. Blockbuster could have stopped mailing late fee bills to customers. They could have eliminated bad debt (uncollected late fees) as a budget item so store managers were not so encouraged to collect it at all cost. They could have wiped out all late fee balances and started fresh with a new, more customer-friendly approach. They could have rewarded customers for returning movies on time with credits to their account. The list was endless. But Blockbuster did none of these. None were big enough ideas for Antioco. It was like he did not understand a fundamental of the business—a store cannot rent what it does not have.

Although Antioco would continue to put a positive spin on the end of late fees (as only he could), Blockbuster's financial position was crumbling, and the cash crunch began almost immediately. As expected, ending late fees broke Blockbuster's supply chain, and it could not afford to buy enough new releases to stock its stores.

Desperation led to attempts to strongarm studios, which, along with layoffs, had always been Blockbuster's chosen way of fixing problems they created for themselves. They needed more DVDs and wanted to spend *less* for them. Some studios cooperated, but others feared not getting paid and demanded cash up-front. Uncooperative studios were punished when Blockbuster arbitrarily reduced purchases or did not buy some titles at all. This, of course, just weakened the stores even more when customers couldn't find the movies they wanted.

By October 2005, nine months after Blockbuster ended late fees, its financial problems had become widely known. There had been multiple layoffs, profits had plummeted, and its stock price was cut in half. There was even talk of impending bankruptcy, five years before it happened. Virtually every benefit Blockbuster claimed would occur by ending late fees had not.

The end of late fees had resulted in a financial crisis, and Nick Shepherd sought to calm the masses in a memo to franchisees. He began with: "These are difficult times for all of us—Blockbuster corporate and franchisees are dealing with an increasingly competitive market." The rest of the memo was a sermon about how, "End of late fees appears to be working," once again citing all sorts of innocuous statistics that bore little relationship to reality and the crisis Blockbuster had created for itself and franchisees. He cited graph after graph explaining how Blockbuster was out-performing franchisees who were not on the program, imploring us to join. In our case, we were having another record year. Customers accepted our decision to continue charging late fees, and we were on pace to post a 10 percent gain in profit. Blockbuster would post a 60 percent decline. Yet they unapologetically implored us to join them in their race to bankruptcy! In their view, we just did not see the big picture.

Shepherd's memo never addressed the biggest issue, which was the broken supply chain caused by ending late fees and the massive out of stocks it created. His memo did not even mention the problem. Perhaps that is because Blockbuster had no solutions.

By the end of 2005, the degree of carnage was fully understood. Rental revenue declined by about $220 million, $150 million more than Blockbuster projected. But the bigger issue was cost for product. In its attempt to reduce massive out of stocks, rental margin declined from 72 percent to 66 percent, which reduced gross profit by $250 million, more than double their expectations. But it was not nearly enough to stop the massive out of stocks caused by ending late fees. Sales never recovered—but even if they had, the end of late fees had destroyed the supply chain and had reduced gross margin to an unsustainable level.

Through massive cost-cutting, layoffs, and ever higher prices, Blockbuster eventually worked its way out of the immediate financial problems caused by ending late fees. But it was only temporary because the stores were weaker than ever—broken. There were fewer reasons than ever to go to Blockbuster. The DVDs you wanted were probably not there—especially new releases, which was about the only reason to go to Blockbuster. What was once its biggest advantage was now a glaring weakness, and a new challenger loomed that would take full advantage. It would come from a most unlikely source.

Shortly before Blockbuster confirmed the end of late fees in late 2004, the franchisees were blindsided by the resignation of Nigel Travis, who had been with Blockbuster since 1994 and had served as President and Chief Operating Officer since 2001. Blockbuster had just completed its final spinoff from Viacom, and Antioco had signed a new 5-year contract.

At 55 years of age, Travis had always wanted to run his own show. With the door shut at Blockbuster, he chose to move on. It turned out to be a great move for him. Blockbuster's *worst* days were ahead of it, but Travis's *best* days were ahead of him. After a successful stint as CEO of Papa John's Pizza, he joined Dunkin Brands in 2009, where he still serves as Executive Chairman. He led a resurgence at Dunkin, taking the company public in 2011 at a share price of $30, which eight years later hit an all-time high of $83, a 175 percent increase, easily outperforming the S&P 500 during that time.

Travis was the franchisees' primary point of contact for over five years and had an exceptionally positive relationship with the ABF board of directors. There were times we did not agree, but Travis was always accessible and was as open with us as he could be in a corporate/franchise relationship. He loved Blockbuster and still says it was the most fun he ever had in business.

With his departure, we had lost our dialogue with a key decision-maker. It was a shock to the system, and we've often wondered: if he had stayed, would things have been different? Would Blockbuster have pursued the end of late fees? When I talked to Nigel about this book, he said he, "Probably would not have eliminated late fees." It wouldn't have been his decision, but perhaps he could have swayed Antioco. We certainly could not.

CHAPTER 10

MCDVD?

"We're about as concerned with McDonald's renting DVDs as they would be if we started frying up hamburgers."

—BLOCKBUSTER SPOKESPERSON, 2004

In 2002, McDonald's (yes, *that* McDonald's) began experimenting with vending machines in its restaurants. One called TikTok (no, not *that* TikTok) sold items like milk, eggs, pantyhose, and even diapers. McDonald's would eventually pull the plug on TikTok, but it continued to test a vending machine it called *Redbox* that rented DVDs for $1 a day. In the summer of 2004, it launched its largest test to date with 100 Redbox DVD kiosks in its Denver restaurants. McDonald's deemed it a success, and Blockbuster privately conceded that its Denver stores had been significantly impacted.

If 100 Redbox kiosks at McDonald's restaurants took sales from Blockbuster, what would happen if thousands of the same machines were at Walmart, supermarkets, drug stores, and convenience stores all over the country? You know that is what happened. Just five years after the initial test in Denver, *DVD kiosks were renting more movies than Blockbuster*, and the company was only months from bankruptcy.

Would you be surprised to learn that Blockbuster had multiple opportunities to participate in the developing kiosk revolution but passed every time? By now, probably not. As had been the case for the entire life of the company, Blockbuster ignored its new competitors—until it was too late.

Greg Meyer was the first to recognize the vast potential of DVD kiosks. He was a Vice President at Lehman Brothers in New York City and had watched as video stores struggled to survive there with smaller stores and the city's notoriously expensive real estate. Then in the late 1990s, it was made worse when a new e-commerce company called Kozmo.com began delivering DVDs to homes via its orange-clad "Kozmonauts" who rode bicycles.

Kozmo.com raised over $250 million in capital and soon expanded its service to other products and eleven more cities. But like most e-commerce companies of the day, Kozmo.com failed. It ceased operations in 2001 but *did* succeed in shutting down so many video stores that it became difficult to rent a DVD in parts of New York City. Ironically, the same stock market bubble that caused Netflix to try to sell itself to Blockbuster in January 2000 had produced a vacuum in the $10 billion movie rental business—in the largest city in the country.

Meyer saw the opportunity and began researching how to fill the void. He even considered buying the franchise rights to open Blockbuster stores, but soon learned that the economics of traditional video stores did not fit with the very untraditional economics of running a retail business in New York City. That realization led him to study the kiosk concept, which up to now had been used mostly in densely populated cities in Europe. He thought less expensive kiosks might be the answer and left Lehman to found DVDXpress with his partner Jason Tanzer.

Very few people know that Meyer was set to deploy his first machine in the retail hub of the busiest office complex in Manhattan—the twin towers of the World Trade Center.

On September 11, 2001, Meyer—who lived just four blocks from the World Trade Center—was about to depart for a 10 a.m. meeting with the leasing agent there when he heard the first plane fly low overhead. Moments later, at 8:45 a.m., it struck the building, and the ground shook beneath him. Like most, he believed it to be an accident, but fifteen minutes later, the second plane hit, and the reality of the disaster became shockingly clear. Had it not been for that tragic day, the first DVD rental kiosk in the U.S. would have been located in the World Trade Center.

Meyer opened his first DVDXpress kiosks in three Duane Reade drug stores in late 2001. He loaded the kiosks with primarily new releases and rented them for $1 a day, which was viewed by most as an absurdly low price. Just like the early Blockbuster stores of the 1980s, customers lined up to rent DVDs. And despite the extraordinarily low price, the kiosks generated exceptional sales volume, and the accompanying lower operating costs produced a business model that worked. Soon, Meyer rolled out dozens of DVDXpress kiosks in drug stores and supermarkets throughout New York and surrounding cities.

The DVD kiosks Meyer deployed are believed to be the first in the U.S., and his new company gained a firm foothold in the movie rental business in the northeast. The success of DVDX-press caught the eye of McDonald's Ventures, a subsidiary of McDonald's that was exploring ways to use vending machines to increase traffic in its restaurants. The aforementioned TikTok vending machines failed, but, just as Meyer discovered, DVD kiosks were a runaway success, and Redbox was born. Soon, McDonald's had installed Redbox in hundreds of restaurants all over the country and later expanded to new territory with kiosks in Safeway supermarkets.

It was in these early days of the DVD kiosk business that Block-buster had the opportunity to join forces with DVDXpress, and later, Redbox. Meyer and McDonald's understood that the speed of rollout was critical. Netflix by-mail was growing rapidly, and the digital delivery of movies loomed on the horizon. They needed to scale up quickly, and who better to partner with than the still undisputed king of home entertainment—Blockbuster. Meyer was the first to make his case.

In February 2004, Meyer made an in-depth presentation to Frank Paci, Blockbuster's Executive Vice President of Finance and Strategic Planning. Meyer brought strong credentials to his proposed partnership. In addition to his investment banking experience with Lehman Brothers, he possessed an MBA from Dartmouth's Tuck School of Business, historically one of the top-ranked programs in the country. He knew how to finance and scale a business, but he knew that could best be accomplished with a recognized brand to accelerate the process. Who better than Blockbuster, which had the resources and was the only national brand in the business?

Meyer's 20-page PowerPoint presentation to Paci spelled out exactly what was to come and how Blockbuster could participate. He explained the kiosk business model, which was beyond the test phase and proven by now. He described how Blockbuster could use kiosks to expand its reach into markets that could not support 6,000-square-foot Blockbuster stores. He described the growth potential of the business, explaining to Paci that he believed it would exceed $500 million in 5 years, which turned out to be exactly right.

Most importantly, Meyer explained how major retailers had already "bought in," and were anxious to install DVD rental kiosks to increase customer traffic to their stores. Soon, he told Paci they would be located in every major supermarket, drug store, and convenience store in the country, which is *exactly* what happened. He succinctly described the situation as a "land grab." There were a relatively small number of retailers that controlled a disproportionally large share of weekly customer traffic—companies like Walmart, Target, Kroger, Safeway, Walgreens, CVS, 7-Eleven, and a few others. The company that partnered with those retailers would win the day. Blockbuster had to act quickly, or it would be left hopelessly behind.

In 2004, Greg Meyer was the authority on the DVD kiosk business. Everyone else was playing catch up, including McDonald's. He sought to combine his expertise with Blockbuster's powerful brand and resources. And he emphasized this: *"DVD rental machines will proliferate. If we don't fill this need, someone else will."* Meyer thought he had made a compelling case and that his proposal had been well received—so much so that he believed a deal was imminent.

But after the meeting, he hit a bureaucratic wall. Repeated follow-up calls were ignored. Paci says he can't remember much from the meeting and that perhaps he talked briefly about it with Nigel Travis, then President and COO, but nothing came of it. They never reached out to Meyer and ignored his repeated requests to meet again.

After more than a year of frustration, Meyer tried another route. By now, Carl Icahn had become Blockbuster's largest shareholder, and Meyer thought he might listen. In May 2005, he sent Icahn a letter that summarized the major points he had made a year earlier in his meeting with Paci. He emphasized once again that major retailers were pressing forward, and Blockbuster could no longer ignore this new distribution method.

When he got no response, Meyer followed up with Icahn's office and was told his letter had been forwarded to John Antioco. But no one from Blockbuster ever spoke to Meyer again. He had done everything he could to educate them about the potential of DVD rental kiosks. It was coming. Ignore it at your peril. But like they had done for every competitor that came before, Blockbuster management did just that. They did not even take the opportunity to *learn* from people like Greg Meyer, who had *pioneered* the concept.

It was around this time that another industry pioneer became involved in the DVD kiosk business. Mitch Lowe had opened some of the first video rental stores in the mid-1980s called Video Droid. They were located in the San Francisco Bay area, which also happened to be near where Netflix—then a small startup—was assembling its first management team in nearby Scotts Valley.

Netflix Co-founder Marc Randolph needed movie expertise and described Lowe as having "the perfect blend of content knowledge and industry knowledge—he loved movies as much as he loved the logistics of renting them."[52]

He recruited Lowe to Netflix in 1998 to help build the company's first inventory. Most importantly, Lowe helped start the culture that so successfully matched Netflix's subscribers to movies they would love. But Lowe also believed that Netflix's major weakness was its inability to provide the instant gratification of renting the movie customers wanted when they wanted it—what Blockbuster *could* do.

Since his early days in the business, Lowe believed that vending machines would someday play a major role in the video rental business. He knew the opportunity to explore them was now; video kiosks could give Netflix customers the movies they wanted instantly, without them having to wait a day or two for delivery. So, in 2003, he persuaded Reed Hastings to allow him to test kiosks for Netflix in Las Vegas. He installed them in Smith's grocery stores and found—just as Greg Meyer had two years prior—that DVD rental kiosks were a winner. Customers loved them. Lowe believed he had found the way to solve Netflix's biggest problem. But Hastings disagreed. "It's a good idea," he said, "but our focus is better spent on our core business."[53]

With the door shut on vending at Netflix, Lowe left to pursue his kiosk dream with McDonald's. And the rest, as they say, is history. Redbox was born; within a few years, the kiosk business was bigger than the store business. Lowe served in various roles at Redbox, including Chief Operating Officer for four years and

President during his last three. By the time he left the company in 2011, Redbox had over 30,000 kiosks, and Blockbuster had filed bankruptcy.

But in its early days, Redbox's immense potential was beyond the scope of McDonald's plans, so, in 2005, Lowe looked for a new partner and offered to sell half the company to Blockbuster for $30 million. But as had been the case for Blockbuster's entire history, it did not understand the threat posed by its new competitor and ignored them until it was too late.[54]

While Blockbuster passed on multiple chances to participate in the rapidly growing kiosk business, another company believed that it was the opportunity of a generation. Coinstar, Inc. was a 14-year-old company that had built a successful business by installing all kinds of self-service machines in retail stores. It had begun with coin exchange machines then expanded to electronic payment solutions and entertainment services. In 2005, its products and services were in 57,000 retail locations, including supermarkets, drug stores, mass merchants, convenience stores, and restaurants.

If ever there was a perfect partner for Redbox, Coinstar was it. It already had relationships with virtually every major retailer in the U.S., as well as the expertise to install and service thousands of self-service vending machines. At the same time Redbox and DVDXpress were trying to partner with Blockbuster, they were also making their pitch to Coinstar. And we know how that turned out.

In the summer of 2005, Coinstar made an investment in DVDXpress that included an option to buy the entire company. Later that same year, in November 2005, they did the same with Redbox. Coinstar then ramped up the growth. Soon Redbox kiosks would be installed in thousands of major retailers in larger cities. DVDXpress was used to fill out the system in smaller markets and retailers. Plus, both Mitch Lowe *and* Greg Meyer were now part of the Coinstar team—the early pioneers of the business who knew it best.

As Blockbuster shunned multiple opportunities to join the DVD kiosk revolution, Coinstar gained control of the two biggest players. It essentially cornered the market. By 2009, they had exercised their right to buy controlling interest in both Redbox and DVDXpress, and this new distribution channel would forever be controlled by one company. To a large extent, Blockbuster's fate had been sealed.

As Redbox rolled out thousands of kiosks every year, Blockbuster management continued to minimize them as a threat to their dominance. How could a bunch of little red boxes compete with their big gleaming stores with thousands of DVDs? The answer spoke to what DVD was. It was a *commodity*, a concept that a long line of Blockbuster executives never grasped, believing instead that DVDs in their stores were somehow worth more.

But the winning companies were those that could profitably deliver the most for the least. Where and how customers rented DVDs was not particularly important if it was convenient. With only 70 titles, Redbox kiosks did not have the most, but because those titles were almost all new releases, every kiosk contained about 90 percent of what Blockbuster customers were looking for—at a fraction of the price.

As to convenience, Redbox was everywhere. Their ubiquitous visibility became their advertising. They did not need to spend money telling people where they were or what they did. That message came through loud and clear every time you went to the grocery store, picked up a prescription, or filled your car with gas. Redbox was *everywhere* you shopped. Their kiosks were located at virtually every major retail destination, sometimes as many as ten at one intersection. There could be four at Walmart, two at Walgreens, two at the local supermarket, and two more at a nearby convenience store—all at the same intersection. Those ten Redbox kiosks could generate sales that exceeded that of a large Blockbuster store.

Redbox was also technologically superior to Blockbuster. DVDs could be searched for and reserved online and returned to any Redbox in the country. Blockbuster had conducted small tests of such services but never fully deployed them. So not only did Redbox have more movies and lower prices, but DVDs were also easier to rent and return.

For Blockbuster, Redbox's entry into the DVD rental business could not have come at a worse time. Every strategy John Antioco had employed in the past few years had either increased the price to rent movies in Blockbuster stores or made them less available. Blockbuster had quite literally made itself a sitting duck to Redbox. The price to rent movies in its stores was higher than ever, and the availability of new releases was worse than ever.

And now, Redbox had changed the game. Millions more DVD new releases would soon flood the market and be priced 75 percent less than the same titles at Blockbuster. And most Redbox kiosks were within walking distance of a Blockbuster store.

So much has been written about Antioco declining Reed Hastings' offer to sell Netflix to Blockbuster that the Redbox story is often overlooked. But Blockbuster's failure to understand the threat posed by DVD kiosks was much more indefensible. Netflix's subscription business model was a new idea, and its focus on renting older movies was a concept Blockbuster had not grasped from its founding. Although a more intellectually curious company might have better understood Netflix's potential, it is not difficult to understand why Blockbuster did not.

But Blockbuster's miss on Redbox seems like reckless negligence. Since its early days, Blockbuster was all about renting new releases—exactly what Redbox did—but for a fraction of the price. When Greg Meyer explained to Blockbuster in 2004 that DVD kiosks would soon be located in every major retailer in the country, he knew of which he spoke. It should have been a call to action. Blockbuster could have built its own kiosk business or joined forces with those who had pioneered it. They had ample opportunity to do both—but did neither.

In 2004, the kiosk business model had already been proven by Meyer and Redbox. The only question was how *big* the business would become. Based on the early tests, it was simple math to determine that the kiosk business would be very big—potentially in the billions. But as had always been the case, Blockbuster ignored ideas other than its own, and by all accounts, did not even take the opportunity to learn what Meyer and other pioneers of the business knew.

So, without a place at the table, Blockbuster could only look on as Redbox exploded. After passing Blockbuster's number of rental transactions in just five years, it passed up *the combined total of all video stores* a year later. As Greg Meyer had warned in 2004, "DVD rental machines *will* proliferate." And just six years later, the kiosk business was bigger than the store business.

For years, Antioco had searched for a silver bullet to save Blockbuster while mostly ignoring the fundamental realities of what renting movies was all about. Now, a simple machine that executed nothing *but* fundamentals would be the final nail in the coffin for Blockbuster. There was no need for flashy stores or gimmicky promotions. Redbox simply delivered more movies—at lower prices—in convenient locations. That was good enough, and soon there would be 40,000 of them. The end was near.

CHAPTER 11

FIXING WHAT'S BROKEN

"I knew if I failed, I wouldn't regret it, but I knew the one thing I might regret is not trying."

—JEFF BEZOS, CEO, AMAZON

As Blockbuster's financial condition spun out of control, our company (Border Entertainment) continued to prosper. Blockbuster's largest direct competitor, Hollywood Video, was struggling and would soon file bankruptcy; we took full advantage as they started to close stores. Netflix by-mail was exploding nationally, but we minimized their impact on our stores by stocking every title our customers asked for, regardless of how obscure. And we fought off Redbox by having better availability of new releases and pricing 90 percent of our inventory below their $1 a day price point. And, of course, we still charged late fees to protect the supply chain.

Instead of weakening our stores with headline-grabbing promotions that defied the laws of common sense, we had used the miracle of DVD to increase sales every year and almost tripled profits. Instead of racing towards bankruptcy, Blockbuster could have done the same. But all attempts to convince John Antioco to reconsider his failed strategies had fallen on deaf ears. He would never listen to anyone outside what had come to be known as the "Boys' Club."

But we were so convinced in our strategy that we asked to buy some of Blockbuster's stores. Even though virtually all of them were in steep decline, we believed we could turn them around, generate a healthy return on investment—and prove a point. Since Blockbuster needed cash, they were open to the idea. So in 2006, we made an offer to buy 24 stores in San Antonio, a large city I was familiar with from my H-E-B days and just an hour's drive from our Austin office.

A quick review of the San Antonio financials had made clear the opportunity. The combined population of our Alaska and El Paso markets was roughly equal to San Antonio, but our profit was almost *four times higher*! To us, the opportunity was obvious, and I was pleasantly surprised when we quickly agreed to the terms of a deal.

Early in the discussions, I told Blockbuster we planned to turn these stores upside down. We would bring back late fees. We would stop selling the Movie Pass. We would rent the newest releases one day at a time. We would drastically lower prices. In other words, we would stop doing everything Blockbuster claimed was *saving* the business—and do the exact opposite. How crazy was that? But if it worked, how would Blockbuster look? How would Antioco look? I asked if he had approved the transaction and was repeatedly told that he had, so we continued to work toward closing the deal.

Despite Blockbuster's precarious financial condition, the acquisition was an easy sell to investors and lenders, some of whom had worked with us before. We contrasted our company's performance with Blockbuster's and explained how we did it. It was a simple strategy of an abundance of product at low prices. That combination produced higher sales as well as higher profit margins. The only question was the customer's reaction to bringing back late fees. Would they understand? We believed having more movies to rent was much more important to customers than no late fees. Our financial partners concurred, and within a few weeks, all parties had agreed on the details of the deal. We went about finishing the documentation—and then the unthinkable happened.

Steve Krumholz, a Blockbuster Senior Vice President, informed me the deal was off. We had spent hundreds of hours and thousands of dollars putting it together, as had our financial partners. I asked for an explanation, but there was none—just that the deal was off.

Steve and I had a great working relationship, and it was obvious that he did not enjoy delivering the bad news. He wanted to get the deal done as much as I did, but it was not to be. It was particularly uncomfortable because he was not free to say why. It was not until several months later at an ABF Board dinner that I learned the truth from Nick Shepherd. Antioco had pulled the plug. Still, he wouldn't say why, but I have always believed it was because our success would have brought his strategy into question. San Antonio was a major market, and we were going to make a big deal out of bringing back late fees and lowering prices, which would have attracted attention from the press. What would happen when we told reporters that charging late fees brought customers *back* to the stores?

It would have been a true test of two completely different strategies. Perhaps Antioco did not want the light shone on the disaster that was developing at Blockbuster. Why am I so certain we would have turned San Antonio around? Because we did exactly that with a similar group of stores later that year.

By 2006, most franchisees had given up. They had followed Blockbuster's failed strategies that resulted in having less but charging more. Customers were leaving Blockbuster stores in droves; sales and profits were plummeting. The only difference between franchisees and Blockbuster is most were not under the financial pressure of debt. So instead of trying to keep lenders off their backs, most were content to ride it out as long as they could and exit before profits turned negative.

We had a different view. We were convinced that most of the damage done to Blockbuster stores was self-inflicted and could be fixed. We just needed the right opportunity to prove it, and since Blockbuster would not sell us stores, we made it known to the franchise community we had an interest in acquiring theirs. We had discussions with several franchisees and finally found the right opportunity.

The franchisee that owned stores in the Rio Grande Valley area of Texas was in severe decline and proposed a sale of its 13 stores.

Taking Blockbuster's lead, they had fully embraced the Movie Pass and, more recently, had stopped charging late fees. Like most other franchisees who followed Blockbuster, sales and profits had plummeted. The stores were on the brink of failure and would soon be forced to close. Store employees were demoralized and knew their days were numbered. But we saw opportunity. It was time to put up or shut up. We agreed on a price and closed the purchase midway through 2006.

The Rio Grande Valley has twice the population of Chattanooga—the market Blockbuster used to test ending late fees. Now we would see if we could resurrect a much larger market that was on the brink of failure by bringing late fees back.

Most thought we were crazy for buying stores when Blockbuster was in such severe decline. Even one of the owners of the stores we purchased told me he did not know why we did it and "wished me luck." But we would never know unless we tried. The first order of business was getting buy-in from the store management team. That started with a marathon meeting with its operations director, Roland Deleon, who oversaw the day-to-day management of all 13 stores. I explained we were totally dedicated to getting the right movies in the stores at the right prices—and yes, we were going to bring back late fees. When I showed him the performance of our stores for the past few years, the strategy was not a hard sell. Most everyone else was in freefall, and we were thriving. He understood and enthusiastically called the transaction a "heart transplant."

It took about three months to fix the stores' depleted inventory, install our business model, and train the store staff on a new way of doing things. Certainly, there was some skepticism, but we implored them to give our strategy a chance. Yes, we are going to bring back late fees. But your stores will have the movies your customers want. We will have more new releases than you have ever seen, and we will have thousands more catalog titles your customers want to watch. And if a customer asks for a title you do not have, just order it. No problem. Most managers bought in but, given what they had been through the last few years, some needed to see it before they would believe it.

Within a week after launch, 20 percent more customers were visiting the stores. Sales immediately shot up 10 percent—and we had not even advertised the change. As word spread and we launched an advertising campaign, sales gains increased to 20 percent. Instead of leaving because we brought back late fees, customers came back—because we had the movies they were looking for. By the end of 2007 (just 18 months into the turnaround), our transformation of the Rio Grande Valley stores produced a 200 percent increase in store cash flow. Yes, it tripled.

We had reversed *every* major strategy launched by Blockbuster in the past few years and it led to explosive growth in sales and profits—in a market that was twice the size of Chattanooga where the end of late fees was tested. Based on the results, I pleaded with Blockbuster to study what we did, but they showed no interest. I also tried to resurrect the San Antonio deal, but that went nowhere as well. Antioco and Shepherd had made their decision. They were going to ride the end of late fees regardless of how customers reacted to bringing them back—in a market twice the size of the one they used to test it.

With no possibility of buying corporate stores, we continued to look at opportunities to acquire more franchise stores. The next opportunity came when we were contacted by a bank that had foreclosed on a 25-store franchise group in the southeast and ousted the owner. In addition to implementing most of Blockbuster's failed strategies, the owner also seemed more interested in living like the "rich and famous" than running a good business. We saw opportunity and talked briefly about buying the stores, but the outstanding debt proved to be an insurmountable obstacle because the bank was unwilling to re-negotiate.

But we believed that if the stores were better managed, the bank could recover much more of its loan balance by running the stores than liquidating them. We used the Rio Grande Valley stores as an example of what could happen if we reversed all of Blockbuster's failed strategies and implemented ours. They agreed, so instead of buying the stores, we entered into a three-way management agreement with the bank, Blockbuster, and new owner Glen Klicker who had been retained from the previous owner to run the stores and was a very capable operator. We followed the same playbook employed in the Rio Grande Valley turnaround and got the same results. Sales and profits improved dramatically, and the stores were re-energized.

By 2007, we had produced dramatic turnarounds in 38 stores that had followed Blockbuster's failed strategies of the past several years. Combined, we were now running 60 stores, and every one of them was outperforming corporate stores—by a wide margin. In terms of growth, the best of the group were the ones we had taken off Blockbuster's failed strategies. It was a small sample among a total of about 5,000 corporate and franchise stores still operating in the U.S. but much larger than the small market (Chattanooga) used to launch what was, by their own admission, the riskiest strategy ever deployed at Blockbuster—the end of late fees.

The immediacy of the turnarounds was a testament to the demand for what we were renting: DVDs. We were *not* irrelevant, as Blockbuster so often told us. DVDs were *still* America's favorite way to watch a movie. In 2007, nothing else came close. Once we got the inventory right and priced it correctly, customers came racing back to the stores. And not a year later but immediately. I repeatedly tried to engage Blockbuster in a discussion about what had happened, but every time I was politely told to go away. From Blockbuster's perspective, Border Entertainment—by now the largest and by far the most profitable franchise group in the system—was irrelevant to the discussion of how best to run a Blockbuster store. Nothing we ever did was of interest to them.

CHAPTER 12

FULL DEATH SPIRAL

"More people would learn from their mistakes if they weren't so busy denying them."

—HAROLD J. SMITH

Just ten minutes after I emailed John Antioco with concerns about Blockbuster's financial condition, he phoned me. "You raise some interesting points," he said. "We should get together to discuss."

It was the summer of 2005. I had not had a substantive business discussion with Antioco for at least five years but not for lack of trying. Given the deteriorating financial condition of the company, I had tried multiple times to talk to him, but Antioco never responded. Not even a, "Thanks for your thoughts." He had totally disconnected himself from the franchise community. I did not expect a response this time either but felt compelled to say something because, just six months into the launch of the end of late fees, Blockbuster was already experiencing a cash crunch and

I believed was in a full death spiral. Antioco had never responded to me before, so why this time?

"I'm taking the company plane to Alaska next week on a fishing trip. It's on my bucket list, and now's the time to go," Antioco explained. "Why don't you join me on the flight up? We can discuss your ideas and visit a couple of your stores in Anchorage." (To be clear, Antioco was not inviting me on the fishing trip.) He went on, "You'll need to arrange your own transportation home, but I hope you can join me on the flight up." I quickly agreed, and we arranged to meet at Love Field in Dallas the following week to depart on the 4,500-mile trip. Here was my chance to talk shop with John Antioco—during an eight-hour flight to Alaska!

When I boarded the Bombardier Challenger the following week, Ed Stead, Executive Vice President and General Counsel, was on the plane, as well as a friend and two teenage boys. Nick Shepherd and Frank Paci were also on the flight, but they were not invited on the fishing trip either. They had been asked to join the business conversation but would be returning to Dallas that same day.

I took a seat across from Antioco's "captain's chair," complete with a satellite phone at his side. As I recall, there were a total of eight passengers on the plane and, evidently, that was enough to warrant a flight attendant. She was there to attend to our every need, including snacks, meals, and drinks. She even brought out a collection of DVDs so we could watch a movie in the final hours of the flight. I felt like I was on an episode of *Lifestyles of the Rich and Famous*.

I came prepared for an in-depth discussion about Blockbuster, and Antioco gave me his polite attention. Our results seemed to interest him but not *how* we did it. I talked about optimum price points and inventory levels. How we were riding the "long-tail" and renting five times more catalog movies than Blockbuster. How we were creating binge-watchers (a novel concept at the time) by renting full seasons of TV shows at very low prices. How we were renting more new releases—but spending half as much to buy them by renting them one day at a time and staying off his revenue-sharing scheme. How we used advertising to build an image of abundance and value. And most importantly, how we were still charging late fees to keep the supply chain intact.

Our company was in the middle of its best year ever because we had built on the strengths Netflix could not duplicate. Blockbuster was in the middle of its *worst* year ever because in its quest to be relevant again, it had consistently tried to be *Netflix* instead of *Blockbuster*. Our stores were three times more profitable than Blockbuster's and growing. Blockbuster's stores had entered a death spiral from which they would never recover.

But early in the discussion, it was evident that Antioco and I were not connecting. His focus was on big ideas meant to generate Wall Street-pleasing headlines—not on dealing with Blockbuster's fundamental issues like poor inventories and high prices. Instead of acknowledging the problems caused by his big ideas, he simply changed the narrative, and it seemed no one in his inner circle would challenge him; my attempts to do so were futile.

When we landed in Anchorage, we headed out to see some stores. Maybe *seeing* our strategy in action would change his thinking. Our stores were radically different from a typical Blockbuster—

especially the ones in Anchorage, which had exceptionally large inventories to support exceptionally high sales. We visited the store on Debarr Road, which, as it turned out, was one of our last stores to close. It was also one of the highest-volume Blockbuster stores in the world. This store had *25,000 DVDs in its catalog inventory alone*, about five times more than the average corporate Blockbuster store. The visual contrast must have been striking to Antioco—but if it was, he did not show it. Hoping numbers would get his attention, I explained that every week, that inventory generated over 10,000 rents—almost *twenty times* the typical Blockbuster. The catalog inventory alone generated more sales than the *total* sales of the average Blockbuster corporate store. Many customers came into our stores with no intention of renting a new release. They were there to continue their discovery of the "long tail." But that was a concept Antioco and Blockbuster *never* understood.

Nothing I said seemed to pique his interest. Perhaps his mind was already on the fishing trip. The only questions I remember him asking were: How was my company capitalized? How was my relationship with my limited partners? Who were my lenders? How much ownership did I have? His only interest seemed to be how the business was meeting my personal financial goals, not how I was running it. As time passed, I began to believe that is where most of his personal focus was as well.

Later, I told the story of the Alaska trip to a franchise friend. He said something I was too naïve to consider at the time. "Don't you get it?" he said. "Antioco just asked you along so he could turn that fishing trip into a business trip—to convert a taxable, personal trip on the company plane into a routine business trip to visit franchise stores in Alaska." If that was the case, it must have been torture to have me along to talk about Blockbuster instead of fishing.

But from 2000 until Antioco left Blockbuster in 2007, I had *one* business discussion with him. It happened to be when he was taking the company plane to Alaska on a personal fishing trip. Regardless of his motivations, I had gotten the opportunity to talk business with John Antioco as the company was entering its final descent into bankruptcy. But I had not influenced his thinking, and we never talked again.

The "fishing trip" flight to Alaska occurred in the summer of 2005, and the end of late fees had been launched in January the same year. It was the latest edition of Antioco's search for the silver bullet—and the results were disastrous. Within months, annual EBITDA (earnings before interest, taxes, and amortization) would fall from $500 million to $138 million.

Ending late fees was a failed attempt to cover up a fundamental mistake made when Antioco did not enthusiastically embrace the miracle that was DVD. Now, innovative competitors were exploiting Blockbuster's weakened stores and rewriting the rules of the game.

Netflix used "never pay late fees again" to attract disgruntled Blockbuster customers and kept them happy by mailing them mostly older movies that Blockbuster did not have. After ignoring them for four years, Antioco finally responded with the in-store Movie Pass, the End of Late Fees, and eventually Total Access by mail with its free in-store rentals. Every program weakened the only advantage Blockbuster had—the ready availability of new releases at attractive prices.

Blockbuster stores were weaker than ever. And now, like a pack of wolves stalking a wounded animal, thousands of Redbox kiosks were surrounding every Blockbuster store in the country and preparing for the final attack. The death spiral was steepening.

Before Antioco fully implemented his failed strategies, Viacom had rid itself of Blockbuster when it sold off its remaining 80 percent stake to the public in September 2004 for a fraction of what it had paid ten years earlier. John Antioco would no longer answer to Sumner Redstone and Viacom. He continued to cast himself as the visionary leader required by changing times, but as the financial fallout from eliminating late fees became known, Blockbuster's share price went into freefall—it dropped by half in just a few months.

But from their Wall Street offices, analysts saw only half the story. The financials were bad, but the stores were considerably worse than they knew. Poor inventory conditions and inflated prices were pushing customers to Netflix, Redbox, and other competitors. Many longtime renters were simply leaving the rental market altogether, preferring to stay home and watch recorded programming on their new DVR. Put simply, there were fewer reasons than ever to go to Blockbuster.

When Antioco challenged dissident shareholders by telling them they did not understand the situation, he was right. But neither did he. Every strategy employed during the past few years had weakened the stores, which were still Blockbuster's only source of profit. Antioco's eloquent descriptions of how Block-buster was seizing the future had become hollow musings of a leader stuck in hope-mode instead of reality. Free cash flow had fallen from $442 million in 2001 to $128 million in 2004—*before* Antioco eliminated late fees, which had only made it worse. Yet Antioco continued to assert that his strategies were "producing the desired results."[55] Perhaps he believed if he said it enough, shareholders would believe him. But the opposite was true.

Enter Carl Icahn, the infamous corporate raider, who was by now Blockbuster's largest shareholder with about 10 percent of the stock for which he had paid $107 million. He did not understand the business either, but he knew a broken company and a weak-ened leader when he saw one. He began a very public debate about how Antioco was running the company. He called him out for several issues, including the elimination of late fees and going on a "spending spree with shareholder's money." Most notable, though, was his criticism of Antioco's $51 million cash and stock compensation package.

Icahn went on to launch an attempt to win three board seats on Blockbuster's seven-member board of directors. The campaign was very public, with both sides claiming the other would ruin the company, but in May 2005, shareholders spoke loudly and clearly. They wanted a change—with 77 percent of the vote, Icahn won a board seat along with his two nominees. It was the ultimate vote of no confidence in how Antioco had run the company the past several years. And even though Icahn's picks occupied only three of the soon-to-be eight board seats, he effectively controlled it.

After the vote, Antioco told shareholders: "I'd be lying if I told you this was a happy day. It is not."[56] To make the vote sting even more, one of the board seats won by Icahn was Antioco's; Antioco threatened to quit if he was not reinstated, which could have triggered the payout of his $50 million severance package. Icahn accused him of "blackmailing" Blockbuster but supported the creation of an eighth board seat to which Antioco was elected, and he continued as Chairman and CEO.

In addition to Icahn, the other two new board members were entertainment industry veterans, Strauss Zelnick and Edward Bleier. Zelnick had held executive positions at Columbia Pictures, 20th Century Fox, BMG Entertainment, and is currently the Chairman and CEO of Take-Two Interactive. Bleier was a 35-year veteran of Warner Brothers Entertainment.

The makeup of the board had radically changed, and the franchise community expected to see a similar shift in strategy. But despite the ongoing and very public squabbles between Antioco and Icahn, little changed. Late fees never came back, the supply chain remained broken, and all Antioco's "big ideas" remained intact. Then, a year later, the extremely expensive Total Access program launched and further weakened the already deteriorating stores. To us, it appeared that Antioco was getting everything he wanted—until early 2007 when Icahn disputed a big bonus Antioco said management earned for 2006 because, "Blockbuster had a very good year."[57]

It is difficult to understand what Antioco meant by "a very good year." In a January 2007 memo to franchisees, he came across as a CEO totally disconnected from reality. In the memo, he began with: "I believe Blockbuster is entering 2007 in a great position."

Few at Blockbuster believed that, and those who did were as delusional as he was. Shareholders were not buying it either, as the stock price was trading at 80 percent off its all-time highs.

Regardless, Antioco took great offense to Icahn's assertion that he had not *earned* his $7.65 million bonus. "It didn't sit right with me," he would say. He went on to say that if Icahn had been more *considerate*, he might have accepted a lesser amount. Instead, he decided to leave, saying he had "been successful enough financially, and it seemed like the right time to transition the business to someone else."[58] To me, that meant Antioco had made enough money for himself, and now it was time to leave. He negotiated an exit compensation package that was about half what he said was contractually owed, then announced in March 2007 he would be leaving by the end of the year. But as it turned out, he left in June when his replacement was hired.

Antioco was Blockbuster's fourth CEO and ran the company from 1997 to 2007, a decade that was, undeniably, its most transformational. He joined the company the same year that the studios began transitioning the business from VHS cassettes to DVD. This change eliminated rental windows, which turned Walmart and other retailers into direct competitors. The convenient size of DVD allowed the birth of Netflix and Redbox, neither of which would have existed with VHS. Home entertainment was also being transformed by the growth of high-definition television, DVRs, direct-broadcast satellite, and of course, the internet, which was benefitting from the rapid expansion of bandwidth to homes. It was a tumultuous period in the business of home entertainment.

But it is important to re-emphasize that when Antioco left Blockbuster in 2007, home entertainment was still *dominated* by the rental and sales of DVD. And in terms of customer transactions, rentals were still much larger than sales. The rental of physical media, a business that Blockbuster had brought mainstream and dominated for two decades, was *still* king. But instead of renting DVDs from Blockbuster, millions had already moved to by-mail where Netflix was king. And millions more were beginning to discover the convenience and low prices of DVD kiosks, where Redbox was king. Blockbuster had failed to participate in this migration, and its failed strategies had encouraged much of it.

When Antioco left Blockbuster in 2007, the streaming Netflix you know today did not exist. And all the other forms of electronically delivered movies via cable and satellite were small players, the total of which was a tiny fraction the size of DVD rental and sales. But under Antioco's watch, enough DVD rental had migrated to by-mail and kiosks that Blockbuster's business model was broken. Its high-cost structure and $1 billion of debt taken on when Viacom spun it off had left it defenseless against lower-cost providers like Netflix and Redbox, both of which seemed to understand the movie rental business better than Blockbuster.

Tragically, Blockbuster had the time, money, and opportunity to have partnered with Netflix, Redbox, DVDXpress, and others. In every case, it had the leverage to strike great deals with pioneers in the changing world of home entertainment. Reed Hastings at Netflix. Mitch Lowe at Redbox. And Greg Meyer at DVDXpress. But every time, Antioco passed.

Blockbuster was also a struggling company when Antioco took charge in 1997 but, within months, he had addressed a few fundamentals in the company's customer proposition that prior management had ignored. He lowered prices and bought more new releases. The fortunes of the company changed almost overnight. To many at Blockbuster and its parent company Viacom, the quick turnaround made John Antioco a hero. Then he disappeared!

The immediacy of the turnaround he engineered seemed to change him. The highly visible John Antioco of 1997-1999 became the invisible John Antioco until he left in 2007. But the challenges were just beginning and, from the perspective of the franchisees, Antioco was totally unengaged. After 1999, just two years after joining Blockbuster, we never interacted with him again on business issues. Never. We only saw him at social functions. Antioco began to take on the image of a celebrity, and the select few members of "The Boys' Club" seemed the only ones who had Antioco's ear. For everyone else, he made brief appearances when it suited his schedule and self-defined celebrity status. More and more, it seemed his carefully crafted image was more important than a business dialogue with the franchise group that represented over a thousand Blockbuster stores in the U.S.

Then we began to hear the same from many in "Ren-Tower," the nickname of Blockbuster's headquarters in downtown Dallas. "Where's John?" became a common theme. It became something of an occasion when there were "John sightings." We heard that Antioco had a bodyguard and a personal driver. And increasingly, it seemed that if one wanted face time with Antioco, it would have to be at his ranch east of Dallas. And then there was that glorious Bombardier Challenger jet complete with a flight attendant that whisked him around the world (and at least one fishing trip). The jet was the ultimate symbol of corporate excess, especially for a company that was in constant financial turmoil.

One of the more notable "John sightings" came in May 2004, shortly before Viacom sold its remaining Blockbuster stock to the public. Blockbuster would be an independent company for the first time in ten years, and that was cause for celebration. Hundreds from all levels of Blockbuster management gathered in Las Vegas, so many that they were housed in multiple hotels. The highlight event was to be an early morning affair. Attendees were told to be in their respective hotel lobbies at 4 a.m. They were not told why and, given it was Vegas, a good many did not go to bed that night.

When the attendees arrived in the lobby that morning, there were dozens of buses lined up on Las Vegas Boulevard to take them somewhere—but no one knew where. They were given Blockbuster-blue jackets because few were prepared for what turned out to be an outdoor event on a chilly morning in the desert. A huge caravan of buses full of Blockbuster management departed the strip and headed to a remote location outside of town. It was still dark when they arrived, and coffee and Chick-fil-A breakfast sandwiches were served. A sea of chairs on the desert floor faced a temporary stage, where an orchestra played welcoming music. As everyone took their seats, they were greeted by various Blockbuster executives. But still, why was it necessary to have this meeting on a cold, dark morning in the Nevada desert?

And then it happened.

As the sun began to rise at 5:30 a.m., the orchestra struck up the theme from *2001: A Space Odyssey*. Then the attendees learned why they had dragged themselves out of bed at 3 a.m. or stumbled from the blackjack tables to board buses to who knew where. It was to see John Antioco ride through the crowd—on a horse—as the sun rose dramatically over the temporary stage. He was equipped with a microphone, and his message spoke to "a new dawn" at Blockbuster. The event was vintage Antioco, the celebrity CEO. Not much about details. Much more about optics. And very much about John Antioco.

To the franchisees especially, Antioco had become much more about image than substance. He sent memos to franchisees after most earnings announcements, touting his strategies and vision for the future. And more than a few times, he announced "bold initiatives" that seemed more like his version of pixie dust than a smartly devised plan. But not one time in his last eight years with Blockbuster did he engage the franchisees in a discussion about the business. It was *always* one-way and from a safe distance.

To many of us, it came as no surprise a few years later when Carl Icahn questioned John Antioco's "work ethic" and said, "His heart didn't seem in it."[59] We had thought the same for years, as had many studio executives that we both dealt with. These executives viewed him as unengaged and either unable or unwilling to talk about the business in any level of detail. One who played eighteen holes of golf with him in 2002 learned that Antioco's preferred discussion topic was his ranch, not Blockbuster or the home entertainment business.

Most surprising is how he was described by the people closest to him. In the research for this book, one described him as "lazy."

Another said: "If you want to rule the world, you've got to show up. John did not show up." When asked why he was never around, another said Antioco believed he was "above it all."

Some told me that Antioco believed himself smart enough to swoop in after being disengaged for weeks at a time, get a crash course on what was happening, fix the problem—and leave—oftentimes after a celebrity appearance at a meeting to fire up the troops. That approach was on full display when he condescendingly scolded franchisees for not agreeing with his decision to end late fees. We had wrestled with Blockbuster on that issue for over a year, and he was never present for any of those discussions. Yet he expected all 1,000 franchise stores to fall in line when he made a celebrity appearance to bless the plan. But by that time, he had lost all credibility with most of us, and his opinion did not matter.

In the 10 years Antioco led Blockbuster, his focus was on topline growth at all costs, which was the genesis of all his "big ideas" and constant search for the elusive silver bullet. But for most of his time at Blockbuster, the only strategy that drove sales was more stores. He opened more than 3,000 stores around the world and doubled sales from about $3 billion to over $6 billion. But during his last 5 years at Blockbuster, same-store sales—the lifeblood of all retail businesses—was the worst in company history. Antioco boasted the company would be ready for whatever came next. But, as had always been the case at Blockbuster, most of the company's capital and attention went into opening more stores. Antioco was no different.

Under Antioco's watch, Blockbuster had spent at least $750 million opening stores and added billions in fixed costs and long-term lease liabilities. It was all in the pursuit of market share because the video rental business had been relatively flat for several years. In fact, Antioco did increase Blockbuster's market share from 25 percent to 40 percent, but at what cost? And how had he positioned it for the future?

All the growth had come by way of more stores or higher prices. On a per-store basis, customer traffic was in almost constant decline, which, bit by bit, was destroying store economics and the company's ability to generate profit. Had it not been for the brief windfall profits that came from lower-cost DVDs in the early 2000s (which Antioco later squandered when he returned to revenue sharing), Blockbuster's problems would have been revealed years earlier.

The foundation for what happened during Antioco's decade reign had been laid in the years prior to his arrival. After rescuing Sumner Redstone and Viacom from total disaster, he had the authority and capital to put the company on a more sustainable course. But instead of redefining the company's mission to match the changing marketplace, he continued down the same path of relentlessly opening stores and never recognizing new threats until it was too late. Blockbuster desperately needed a fully engaged leader, one who had an unrelenting curiosity about what motivated its customers to rent movies so it could adapt to the inevitable changes to come. I never believed that was what Antioco was about, and neither did others who knew him better than I.

Antioco still points to his unprofitable Total Access by-mail business as Blockbuster's path to the future. But the harsh reality was that even if it had eventually turned a profit, it would not have been nearly enough to cover the bloated cost of operating over 8,000 stores, most of which had several years of lease obligations and were only marginally profitable (and becoming less so by the day).

When Antioco left Blockbuster in June 2007, there were about 8,300 stores, more than half of which were in the U.S. Annual sales were trending at about $5.5 billion—still almost double that of the year he arrived a decade earlier. Yet, the company was barely profitable, and sales trends were the weakest in its history. Blockbuster could not service its debt, and its stock was trading at one-third of its all-time high. And because of its precarious financial condition, the company didn't have access to new capital, which would be necessary for any hope of survival. Yet Antioco insisted Blockbuster was well-positioned for the future, and just three years later, would blame the company's failure on his successor.

CHAPTER 13

ONE LAST CHANCE

"There are hundreds of companies that are traditionally great brands but had to transform themselves into a new business model."

—JIM KEYES, BLOCKBUSTER CEO 2007-2010[60]

When Jim Keyes arrived at Blockbuster as its fifth CEO in June 2007, I felt like I was alone on a deserted island. Having almost tripled profits over the past decade, our company, Border Entertainment, was in the middle of its best year ever. All 700-plus employees in our company were energized and optimistic. In stark contrast, corporate Blockbuster was a confused and demoralized company that was on the brink of financial failure.

There were still about 800 franchise stores open in the U.S., but owners seemed more interested in getting out of the business than fixing it. I felt so disconnected from the organization, I had resigned from the ABF board of directors. There was no point attending meetings to hear corporate executives and fellow franchisees discuss a declining business with which I was unfamiliar, especially since no one had shown much interest in how our company continued to thrive.

There were also growing concerns about Blockbuster among Wall Street analysts, but high prices were camouflaging how bad it had become. It was much worse than they knew, but even I did not recognize how bad it was until a couple of years later when I obtained more detailed financial information as part of the bankruptcy proceedings. I had never seen individual store financials down to the bottom line until then and what I learned was astonishing. Our 16 franchise stores in Alaska were generating more profit than the Blockbuster stores in 28 other states! To be clear, when all 50 states were ranked by the total profitability of Blockbuster stores in each state, Alaska ranked 21st, even though it ranked a distant 48th in population.

To put this in better perspective, Pennsylvania had 12.7 million people and 93 Blockbuster stores. Alaska had only 700,000 people, but our 16 Blockbuster franchise stores generated 25 percent more profit than their 93. The gap between what Blockbuster could have been and what it had become was startling. In my 25 years at Blockbuster, it was the most revealing statistic I ever saw. Blockbuster had destroyed its stores in pursuit of the ever-elusive silver bullet, always believing the next gimmicky solution would be the big fix. Instead of managing the fundamentals of the business and building on the many strengths of Blockbuster stores, it had systematically wrecked them.

Blockbuster was in critical condition when Jim Keyes arrived in 2007. But I believed there was still time to save the company, especially given our recent success turning around 35 franchise stores by reversing all of Antioco's failed strategies. There was no reason Keyes could not do the same. But what happened during the next three years reminded me of my days at H-E-B. Even though H-E-B is one of the most successful retail companies in the world, their executive team always struggled to understand the movie rental business.

Video Central was successful because H-E-B gave Craig Odanovich and his management team broad authority to run it like a video rental company—*not* like a grocery company. We had their unwavering support, but talking to any H-E-B executive about the movie rental business was always awkward. They were grocery people and did not understand it. The proof came in the years following Hollywood Video's acquisition of the Video Central stores. H-E-B still had over 40 successful video rental departments in their grocery stores, but since most of the video management team had left for Hollywood Video or other pursuits, they turned the management of them over to traditional grocery people. Within two years, performance deteriorated, and they were all closed.

Video rental was drastically different from more traditional retail, and even the best retail managers struggled to understand it. I believed the same was true of Jim Keyes. His instincts were to *sell* things—not *rent* things, and that is not what Blockbuster or any video rental store was about. He did not have much time to learn that; before he could, forces out of his control pushed the company into bankruptcy.

Jim Keyes had spent his entire career in the convenience store business, most recently as CEO of 7-Eleven. He came with a plan to save Blockbuster, but despite what he and so many others believed, running Blockbuster was unlike any other kind of retail business. That had been demonstrated repeatedly over the years. I tried to influence his thinking when he arrived at Blockbuster but was unsuccessful. I was a 60-store franchisee among all the increasingly impatient constituents whose support he needed more than mine. These included his board of directors, shareholders, lenders, the Hollywood studios, and others. I was way down the list and never broke through.

To those outside Blockbuster, it must have appeared like Keyes walked into the opportunity of a lifetime. He took charge of a struggling American icon with nowhere to go but up. Blockbuster was *still* the dominant force in home entertainment with over 8,000 stores and annual sales of $5.5 billion, down just 8 percent from its peak three years prior. Departing CEO John Antioco claimed Blockbuster was perfectly positioned for the future, mostly because its DVD-by-mail business had grown faster than Wall Street's favorite Netflix over the last year. And it would still be years before digital delivery of movies to homes would become a major factor. As a bonus, Blockbuster's largest competitor—Movie Gallery/Hollywood Video—would file Chapter 11 bankruptcy and close over a thousand stores a few months after Keyes arrived. It must have appeared to be a made-to-order turnaround opportunity. But those of us on the inside knew Blockbuster was in deep trouble.

Hollywood Video had been in hyper-growth mode since 1994; by 2003, it had opened almost 2,000 stores in the U.S. But, like Blockbuster, its weak operating discipline and growth-at-all-costs strategy caused financial strain as Netflix by-mail gained market share. The situation was made worse by a $100 million acquisition of internet startup Reel.com that never fulfilled its promise. Hollywood Video subsequently put itself up for sale and was purchased in 2005 by Movie Gallery, which had 2,500 stores located in mostly smaller, rural markets. Movie Gallery failed to successfully assimilate the larger Hollywood stores, and the company experienced immediate financial difficulty. In 2007, just 2 years after the acquisition, Movie Gallery reorganized in bankruptcy and closed over 1,000 stores. But difficulties continued. It re-filed and closed all remaining stores in 2010. The combined annual sales of Movie Gallery/Hollywood Video was over $2.5 billion, but Blockbuster was in such a state of disarray during this period, they failed to take full advantage of the demise of their largest brick-and-mortar competitor.

Jim Keyes had served in several executive roles in strategic planning and finance at 7-Eleven on the way to becoming Chief Financial Officer in 1996 and was named Chief Executive Officer in April 2000, a position he held until he left the company when it was taken private in 2005. The year before he became CEO, 7-Eleven's stock price had dipped as low as $2.75 per share. Five years later, Seven-Eleven Japan Co. Ltd. paid $37.50 per share to take the company private, a gain of over 1,200 percent under Keyes's watch. During that same 5-year period under John Antioco, Blockbuster's share price had fallen by over 50 percent.

Keyes attributes much of his success at 7-Eleven to upgrading its technology. "Pay-at-the-Pump" was one of the first initiatives he championed in the late 1980s. Later, he transitioned the company to full barcode scanning, a technology it had been slow to adopt and which brought drastic improvement to its inventory management.

By 1995, when Keyes became Chief Financial Officer, these advancements helped 7-Eleven produce 40 straight quarters of positive same-store sales growth, a rare feat in any business and unheard of in retail. Keyes's track record of success was undeniable, and he left the company in 2005 at the age of 50 with a $64 million compensation package. Still young and with a sterling track record overseeing a giant base of small stores all over the world, he seemed an ideal choice to bring Blockbuster back from the brink of failure.

Keyes won the head job at Blockbuster over Antioco's choice, Nick Shepherd, its President and Chief Operating Officer at the time. Three years later, under Keyes's watch, Blockbuster filed bankruptcy, and he has been targeted by those in the Antioco regime ever since, who conveniently blame him for Blockbuster's demise. Most recently, they used a 2019 documentary film called *Netflix vs. the World* as a platform to cast blame, while never assuming any of the responsibility for Blockbuster's debilitated condition when Antioco left in 2007. The film concludes that Total Access was propelling Blockbuster into the future and, had Antioco not left over the bonus dispute with Icahn, Blockbuster would have likely won the battle with Netflix. Antioco, Shepherd, Evangelist, and others gleefully support that conclusion. Evangelist goes so far as to call Antioco's dispute with Carl Icahn over his bonus "the day Blockbuster died," and believes Blockbuster would have reigned supreme had Antioco remained in charge.

The issue of who is responsible for Blockbuster's demise is far more complex than conveniently blaming Antioco's successor. The Blockbuster that Jim Keyes inherited had a multitude of problems, as evidenced by the stock price—under Antioco's watch, it had fallen over 80 percent from its all-time high five years earlier. The company had broken debt covenants several times, and it happened again the week Keyes arrived. Blockbuster had already experienced repeated cash crises, had multiple layoffs, and frequently had to plead with the studios for financial assistance to stock its stores with movies. For years, Blockbuster had bounced from one crisis to the next, mostly because instead of John Antioco's "big ideas" making things better, every one of them made things worse.

The Blockbuster Jim Keyes inherited is best described by the following:

- Even though 50 million customers were *still* visiting Blockbuster stores every month—*seven times more* than the 7 million subscribers Netflix had at the time—Antioco's failed strategies had so buried Blockbuster under a bloated cost structure, the company was barely profitable.
- Blockbuster had $1 billion of debt, all of which was due in the next three years. It would have to be paid or refinanced, but in its current financial condition, there was no clear path to do either.
- With over 3.5 million subscribers, Total Access was still unprofitable. And even though Evangelist claimed it would break even at 5 million subscribers, it was impossible to quantify the damage that millions of free rentals was inflicting on the stores.
- Blockbuster had store lease liabilities of *$2.4 billion*, $650 million of which was due after 2010—one year *after* Blockbuster eventually filed bankruptcy. Killing the stores in favor of a Netflix by-mail clone was never an option.

- Redbox had over 7,000 kiosks and was opening thousands more every year. But even more importantly, they had already forged relationships with virtually every major retailer in the country, essentially cornering the market.

While it may be true that Blockbuster had nowhere to go but up when Keyes arrived, how to *get there* was a different matter. The company had seemingly insurmountable hurdles, and just 15 months after Keyes took the job, it got much worse. Lehman Brothers filed bankruptcy on September 15, 2008, in what is still the largest bankruptcy filing in U.S. history. Financial markets froze and severely limited Blockbuster's options to refinance its debt. The financial crisis led to what has become known as the Great Recession, and consumer spending plunged. Even though Blockbuster and the video rental industry had successfully weathered recessions in the past, this one was different. Almost overnight, sales plummeted 20 percent, the largest decline in its history.

The same happened at our company's franchise stores. The resulting decline in profit was so severe, we had to refinance our remaining debt. We successfully did so and profitably ran the business for another 10 years. But in its weakened state, Blockbuster was not so fortunate. With fewer and more expensive refinancing options and permanently lost sales, the Great Recession had dealt Blockbuster a near-fatal blow.

Later, it was dealt another unexpected setback. Closed stores from the Movie Gallery/Hollywood Video bankruptcy had brought improved sales to Blockbuster, but it also raised credit concerns among the studios that had been burned twice by the

Movie Gallery bankruptcy filings: once with the initial Chapter 11 filing in 2007 and then again when it liquidated in 2010. Blockbuster's financial condition was so fragile, it relied on extended dating from studios to survive. But not wanting to repeat the experience from Movie Gallery's problems, studios began to shorten payment terms to Blockbuster. Some studios even demanded cash up front. This sucked much-needed working capital from the company, further weakening its already fragile financial condition.

Jim Keyes's style was decidedly different from John Antioco—this was instantly evident from his compensation package. While Antioco chose to leave the company over a disputed $7.65 million bonus, Keyes took a modest salary and invested $3 million of his own money in Blockbuster stock. There would be no corporate jet, no bodyguard, and no driver. Nor did Keyes play the role of the "celebrity CEO." He was highly accessible. The franchisees had more face time with Keyes in his first year than the entire 10-year reign of Antioco. We heard the same from rank-and-file corporate employees who said Keyes seemed to be "everywhere."

Keyes came to Blockbuster with a plan to revive the company but spent most of his first few months putting out fires. The financial condition of the company was much worse than he thought, and holdovers from the Antioco regime had difficulty accepting the reality of the situation. Instead of a disciplined and accountable company, Keyes found one that had been trained to support the "gimmick of the day," the latest of which was Total Access, which he believed was losing at least $100 million a year. Before that, it was the end of late fees, which sucked over $300 million of profit out of the company that never came back. The result was a company that was barely profitable and in precipitous decline.

Keyes did not believe Total Access could ever be profitable and understood the damage being inflicted on the stores was incalculable. Over the objections of Nick Shepherd and Shane Evangelist, he throttled the program back by raising the price and pushing subscribers to a less expensive version that did not offer free in-store exchanges. Most franchisees and I applauded this decision because we understood that giving away millions of free movies in the stores was unsustainable.

But Shepherd and Evangelist vehemently objected to Keyes's plan to charge more for free in-store exchanges. They believed the better option was to exit the by-mail business by accepting the offer Netflix had made to buy Total Access for over $700 million, a deal they believed was still on the table. Keyes says that offer was not available, but given the circumstances, it is likely some sort of deal could have been reached. Subscriber acquisition was expensive, and the immediate addition of 3.5 million Total Access subscribers could have attracted a substantial price from Netflix, if not the original $700 million offer, surely something close to it. The proceeds could have improved Blockbuster's financial condition and bought critical time to implement the other components of his strategy.

But selling Total Access to Netflix did not fit Keyes's plan to be a player in every channel of home entertainment distribution, so he did not pursue it. Then not surprisingly, when he raised the price for Total Access's free in-store rentals, subscribers left in droves and returned to Netflix, which gained 3 million subscribers over the next 18 months for a total of over 9 million. Blockbuster's by-mail business declined to less than 2 million. Without free DVDs from stores, Total Access could not compete with Netflix. The mass exodus confirmed what everyone knew. Most Total Access subscribers came for the free movies. When asked to pay a fair price for them, they left.

Shepherd and Evangelist believed Keyes's decision to pull back from Total Access was destroying the future of the company and resigned a few months later. When John Antioco learned of Keyes's plan, he gleefully boasted from a safe distance that he bought Netflix stock. "I bought a LOT of Netflix stock," he said as he laid all the blame for Blockbuster's eventual failure on Keyes.[61]

But Keyes had brought much needed fiscal discipline and accountability to Blockbuster. With fewer Total Access subscribers, more new releases were available for customers to rent in stores, and he was able to better manage costs. Sales stabilized in 2007 and 2008 and profits were steady for a brief period. Carl Icahn cheered: "There was little question that Blockbuster was sick and needed the new medicine that has been administered by Jim Keyes and his team. They are to be highly congratulated."[62] And remarkably, Keyes successfully refinanced a portion of Blockbuster's debt that was due in 2009. Even with the horrible effect of the Great Recession, Keyes believed he had stabilized a sinking ship and had positioned it for the future.

Perhaps the biggest threat to Keyes's plan to bring Blockbuster back from the brink was the runaway success of Redbox, which, as we know, was rapidly installing thousands of DVD rental kiosks all over the country. Although Netflix had garnered most of Blockbuster's and Wall Street's attention the past several years, Redbox had become the more immediate threat to the company's deteriorating financial condition.

While Redbox grew during Antioco's final years at Blockbuster, he did nothing to slow them down, preferring to devote all his attention to Netflix. When Keyes arrived, Redbox already had 7,000 kiosks installed, which rented as many movies as at least 700 Blockbuster stores. And within a couple of years, there would be over 25,000 Redbox kiosks in operation.

Redbox was a greater threat because they rented mostly new releases, which was about the only reason to go to a Blockbuster store. Every newly installed Redbox kiosk took even more customers directly from Blockbuster, where new releases were priced four times higher. Keyes wanted to cover all distribution channels, so developing a kiosk plan of his own had to be part of his strategy. But with little time or money to mount a Blockbuster-managed initiative, he turned to a partner to both finance and run it. In August 2008, 14 months after he became CEO, Keyes announced a partnership with NCR Corporation to roll out DVD vending machines that would be called Blockbuster Express.

Blockbuster Express would be the company's latest edition of "too little, too late." Redbox already had most of the country's major retailers under contract and had spent five years perfecting its system. The Blockbuster/NCR relationship was dysfunctional and years behind. NCR financed it, managed it, and paid Blockbuster a royalty to use the brand. Eventually, 10,000 Blockbuster Express kiosks would be deployed, but most were in subpar locations as compared to Redbox, and all were technologically inferior. As a result, Blockbuster Express never posed a serious threat to Redbox or created a financial benefit to Blockbuster.

Even though many of Keyes's early decisions brought the ire of the holdovers from Antioco's management team, most franchisees believed he did what he had to do to stave off certain bankruptcy. But he had been frustratingly silent about his long-term plans for Blockbuster stores. They were broken. What did he plan to do about it? Then six months after his arrival, he revealed his plan. There had been no input from franchisees and, as we later learned, not a lot from Antioco's holdovers either. It was mostly the product of Keyes and other new members of his executive team, none of whom had any experience in the movie rental business.

Keyes's plan was comprehensive and cleverly called "Rock the Block." But franchisees were less than thrilled. It was almost entirely a rehash of old ideas, most of which had been tried countless times and failed. The plan was conceived by well-meaning people, but they did not understand the movie rental business. Given the company's weakened condition, perhaps they believed that was an advantage. Not much had gone right at Blockbuster for years, so perhaps they thought a large dose of new ideas from outside the company was needed.

But there were certain truths of what a Blockbuster store could be and what it could not be. They did not seem to understand either. Keyes and his team were in the black hole of the Johari Window. They did not *know* what they did not *know*.

There was not one franchisee who believed Keyes's "Rock the

Block" plan addressed the biggest problems. Blockbuster's financial condition was critical, and fundamental issues needed to be addressed immediately. But Keyes's plan tinkered around the edges and did not deal with the two most urgent issues. First, late fees had to be charged to repair the broken supply chain and reduce cost. And second, Blockbuster had to disconnect itself from the outrageously expensive and inefficient revenue-sharing deals with the studios.

The elimination of late fees had wiped out at least $300 million in profit and destroyed Blockbuster's biggest advantage against Netflix—better availability of new releases. It was undeniably Blockbuster's biggest problem, and the *only* way to fix it was to bring back late fees. Keyes agreed in principle but did not believe he had the freedom to bring them back immediately because of potential backlash from shareholders who did not understand why they were necessary. We tried to convince him that he had no choice. He must take a stand against his board, shareholders, and anyone else who stood in the way. "Do it now!" we implored. "When they see the results, they will understand." But he never did, until it was too late a couple of years later.

He also agreed that the current revenue-sharing deals with the studios were inefficient and too expensive. But instead of eliminating them and buying DVDs at straight wholesale cost, he believed he could negotiate *true* revenue-sharing deals with terms favorable to Blockbuster. We explained we had been dealing with the same studio people as Blockbuster for the last 25 years. They would never change. And despite Keyes's best efforts to convince them otherwise, they did not. The prohibitively expensive revenue sharing programs stayed in place. And without late fees to repair the supply chain, Keyes's only way to improve new release availability was to spend more money, which he did. By the end of his first year, rental gross margin fell to its lowest level in the history of the company.

His other initiatives for the stores were a list of recycled ideas that had been tried over and over but failed every time. Convinced he could make it work, Keyes told us that just because it had failed before does not mean he could not do it successfully this time. We could not argue with his logic, but unfortunately, every one of those recycled ideas failed—again. He painfully learned that Blockbuster customers do not come to stores to buy televisions, phones, iPods, cameras, toys, or video games. And they do not come to Blockbuster to sit at a soda fountain or gather with friends over coffee to read books and magazines.

It took me back to all the testing we did at H-E-B. We tried it all in the Video Central stores, but none of it worked. For years, I had watched others at Blockbuster do the same time and time again and get the same results. Most notable was Bill Fields, who had tried it 10 years earlier and almost destroyed the company in the process. But Keyes had to prove it to himself, and soon he learned what we had known for years. Blockbuster customers came to rent movies and buy snacks to enjoy while they watched them—the same mindset they had when going to movie theaters. As much as we may have wanted it to be otherwise, it was not and never would be.

To make matters worse, in the process of re-testing what we all knew would not sell, precious space was taken away from the DVDs Blockbuster customers came to rent. Catalog sections were shrunk to alarmingly small areas of the store. Keyes eliminated many of the movies we were convinced had helped our stores in Alaska and Texas hold their own against Netflix and Redbox. But Keyes did not consider them important and even mocked Netflix for building its business around them. He said: "I've been frankly confused by this fascination that everybody has for Netflix...I don't care how many movies are available to me. As a personal taste as a customer, I want to watch the new stuff, so whether we have 10,000 movies or 200 movies doesn't matter if I don't want to see any of the movies that we have... our assortment is heavily weighted toward newer releases and mainstream staple titles."[63]

Perhaps that statement was meant to appease disgruntled shareholders, but, regardless, it ignored a growing trend. As we had discovered in our stores, the expansion of customer tastes described in Chris Anderson's book *The Long Tail* was very real. We were renting more catalog titles than ever, five times more than the average Blockbuster store. The more we stocked, the more we rented. But most importantly, Netflix was by now Blockbuster's largest competitor and had come to be so by renting the very titles Keyes was eliminating. Reed Hastings had been open about their strategy, perhaps because he knew Blockbuster would never grasp the concept. Yet Keyes was convinced he could carve out a profitable place in the movie rental business by focusing almost entirely on new releases. We knew that was not possible, and it was painful to watch him turn away from what was an essential component of a successful Blockbuster store.

Throughout his time at Blockbuster—and despite disagreements with franchisees—Keyes remained open to discussing these and many other issues. It was a welcomed change from every prior CEO, all of whom rarely spoke with franchisees. When I continued to speak of our success and how product management was the key, he arranged a half-day meeting for me to present our business model to him and his product management team. I walked them through our sales and profit history and how we did it, complete with inventory assortment and how it rented and generated profitable revenue. I described a completely different way to manage the business—how we generated more sales and more profit but spent far less doing so. I contrasted all our results with theirs and, by now, the disparity was astounding. Our stores were about 5 times more profitable than theirs.

I had been at Blockbuster for 15 years, and this was the first time I had been asked to explain exactly how we did it—how we had continued to grow our business when the rest of the organization was in decline. I was thankful for the opportunity, but I was not able to change Keyes's mind. He told me that because we were a small company, our methods were not scalable. I never understood that comment. That is what computers are for. I explained I could do the same for Blockbuster with a few programmers. It was not that hard. But nothing I said swayed him. As had always been the case with Blockbuster, our company was in a completely different business, one they never understood. At least Keyes had tried. That is more than I could say for every other Blockbuster executive with whom I worked.

In 2007, the same year Keyes joined Blockbuster, Netflix started dabbling in a business that in a few years would change home entertainment forever—streaming. It began as a free add-on to its DVD-by-mail service but had limited appeal because in those days, streaming movies to the living room television was almost impossible. Streamed movies could only be watched on a computer monitor, and later, mobile devices like the iPhone and iPad. It would be years before Roku and smart TVs would make streaming a big-screen event in family rooms around the world.

To make matters worse, most of the content on Netflix's new streaming service was a hodgepodge of mostly secondary titles. The novelty of watching movies instantly was interesting, but without great content, it would be difficult for Netflix's new streaming service to pose a threat to traditional television. Jeff Bewkes, then CEO of Time Warner, famously derided Netflix by comparing it to the Albanian army trying to take over the world. "I don't think so," he would say. And had it not been for what happened over the next few years, he may have been right.

In what has been lamented by many as the most damaging mistake in its history, Hollywood licensed a treasure trove of content to Netflix for what turned out to be a bargain price. In October 2008, Starz licensed its catalog to Netflix for $30 million a year. Two years later, Epix did the same, but by then, the price had risen to $200 million a year. Those deals included thousands of movies and television shows from the likes of Disney, Sony, Paramount, MGM, Lionsgate, and others. Combined, it represented about 60 percent of all movie titles in the vaults of the Hollywood studios. It was considered "found money" by the studios, paid to them by an upstart streaming service too small to matter. But those two deals accelerated Netflix's growth and brought over 12 million new subscribers in just three years.

Unwittingly, Hollywood had created its biggest competitor, and it has been playing catchup ever since. Barry Diller, who ironically is the one who lost the bidding war with Viacom to buy Paramount in 1994, describes it this way: "They [Hollywood studios] were all asleep to it during the early ascendance of Netflix. Now they've woken up to it, and it has slipped away from them and is never to be regained."[64]

But what if those deals had never happened? What if *Blockbuster* had bought the streaming rights for Starz and Epix instead of Netflix? They could have, and almost did.

Jim Keyes's predecessors labeled him as the CEO who took Blockbuster backward by focusing exclusively on its stores instead of internet-based businesses. Shane Evangelist derided Keyes's 7-Eleven background when he condescendingly commented that he "...certainly couldn't deliver a Slurpy through a digital connection."[65] But Antioco's regime had done almost nothing to prepare for the digital future. That was, after all, how Evangelist got the job to start Blockbuster's first internet business. He could at least spell it.

But Keyes had a plan to move Blockbuster into the digital world. Its merits can be argued, but it was far more comprehensive than anything Antioco had put forth in his 10 years as CEO. It began with Keyes's purchase of a website called Movielink in August 2007, just two months after he arrived. Movielink was a joint venture of most of the Hollywood studios, including Twentieth Century Fox, Warner Brothers, Universal Studios, Paramount Pictures, MGM, and Buena Vista Pictures (owned by Disney). It rented and sold movies on demand, but for a variety of reasons, the site never gained traction, and the studios took a loss when they sold it to Blockbuster for $20 million.

Although the studios had failed in their first attempt to join the march to the digital future, Movielink did contain the infrastructure necessary to do so. And now Blockbuster owned it. But it needed content, and they had the opportunity to acquire it when they were presented with the chance to buy the rights to the very same content from Starz and Epix that was later acquired by Netflix. And they could have done so for $100 million a year, less than half what Netflix paid.

Throughout its history, Blockbuster passed on opportunities that could have changed its future for the better, most famously when Antioco rejected an offer to buy Netflix for $50 million—then later when they passed on opportunities to partner with both DVDXpress and Redbox. But in those cases, as well as all the others, its financial ability to strike a deal was never a factor. Blockbuster had plenty of money.

But this time, in mid-2008, it did not. The company was short on cash, its stock price had fallen 80 percent, and it had broken debt covenants multiple times. Raising new capital was not an option. So, presented with an opportunity that could have changed the course of entertainment history, Keyes had to say, "No." Blockbuster was in such a weakened financial state, it couldn't afford it. But Netflix could, and from that point forward, Reed Hastings's company would rewrite the rules of home entertainment.

A little more than a year after Keyes's first financial fire drill to stabilize Blockbuster, the Great Recession had deepened the sales decline, and he was again trying to save the company from bankruptcy. But his initiatives had made the stores even more dependent on new releases, and that required cooperation from the studios, who were becoming more concerned than ever about Blockbuster's ability to pay. They began shortening payment terms and, in desperation, Blockbuster had to pledge its 450-plus stores in Canada as collateral to keep DVDs coming. Canada had some of the best stores in the company, but soon the studios would seize them as a part of the bankruptcy process and close them all down.

Although Keyes continued to speak positively about Blockbuster's future, sales continued to decline, and the noose was tightening. He tried to stabilize sales by raising prices, which, of course, made matters worse. He also brought back late fees, but it was too late. Blockbuster was still generating over $3 billion in annual sales, but the company was so buried under a mountain of fixed costs from too many stores and a load of debt, it was just a matter of time before its creditors had had enough. That happened on September 23, 2010. The mighty Blockbuster filed for Chapter 11 bankruptcy in a federal bankruptcy court in New York City.

In the months leading to bankruptcy, Greg Meyer, who first encouraged Blockbuster to enter the DVD kiosk business, had become one of Blockbuster's largest shareholders; he accumulated over $1 million in Blockbuster stock. (For the past several years, he had continued to run DVDXpress for Coinstar but had recently left the company.) At less than $1 a share, Blockbuster was priced for bankruptcy, but Meyer was convinced it was a good investment because he believed Keyes would find a way to avoid it. Meyer intended to remain a passive investor, but when Blockbuster's financial condition continued to deteriorate, he went directly to Keyes with recommendations to save the company.

Meyer told Keyes that kiosks could still play a pivotal role in saving Block-buster; he also revived the idea of selling or licensing its by-mail business. And commenting on behavior that I had observed for years, he called Blockbuster out for being more interested in criticizing competitors than learning from them, which he attributed to its "culture of complacency."

Keyes rejected his ideas, but Meyer did not give up. A board seat was open because Carl Icahn had recently thrown in the towel and resigned his. As one of Blockbuster's largest shareholders (larger than any board member except Keyes) and with more firsthand experience in the video rental business than the rest of the board combined, Meyer believed he was imminently qualified to fill that seat. But again, he was rejected and told to go away.

So convinced his ideas could help Blockbuster stave off bankruptcy, Meyer launched a proxy fight to win a board seat, and a very public debate ensued. Blockbuster called Meyer "naïve" and nothing more than an "unemployed consultant." They called DVDXpress a "nominal" company as compared to the multi-billion-dollar Blockbuster; they were seeking to minimize Meyer's experience, although the rest of the board had none. Instead of encouraging a constructive debate with an industry veteran, Keyes did everything he could to shut it down.

But just as had happened when Icahn won over the shareholders five years prior, Meyer did the same. When it became apparent that he would comfortably win the proxy vote, Keyes asked him to join the board. As was so often the case, outsiders (in this case, passive shareholders) seemed more open to new ideas than Blockbuster's tightly controlled manage-ment team. But Meyer soon learned that it was too late. Two months after he attended his first board meeting in June 2010, Blockbuster elected to miss a debt payment, which triggered the bankruptcy process.

Greg Meyer was first rejected in 2004 by Antioco's management team. Five years later, he was rejected again, this time by Keyes. Meyer pio-neered DVD kiosks, the very business that had inflicted the final and fatal blow to Blockbuster. After being bought out by Coinstar, he joined their management team, which of course also owned Redbox, a company that by now was renting more movies than Blockbuster. But he was dismissed out of hand as "naïve" and not having enough experience to provide a meaningful contribution to the company.

Meyer's story is emblematic of what I experienced at Blockbuster for 25 years. Leadership changed, but the culture never did. Ideas that did not come from within were never given serious consideration—until it was too late.

Early in the bankruptcy process, Blockbuster indicated that the senior bondholders had already agreed to a quick reorganization. They would restructure its $675 million in senior debt, close unprofitable stores, and resume normal operations. But the stores were in worse shape than ever. As we watched the stores continue to decline, it became obvious that, without a total change in strategy, liquidation would be the only option. We could either stand by and watch or try to be part of the solution. We chose the latter.

With Keyes's permission, I led a group of franchisees who still believed there was something to save. And we were 100 percent certain the stores were worth more operating than liquidated—if run correctly—and we believed we were the ones to do it. We contacted the largest debt holders, explained how we ran the business differently, and how Blockbuster stores could do the same. They listened, but none understood the potential. They seemed tired of it all, and I believed they had already made up their minds to close all the stores.

Since the current lenders did not seem interested in saving the stores, we found our own investment banker and made the rounds of major financial institutions in New York City. Perhaps they would be interested in buying Blockbuster out of bankruptcy. We even met with two of Carl Icahn's senior people, Vincent Intrieri, a Sr. Vice President, and Icahn's son, Brett. They were already angry, having lost almost all their $185 million investment in Blockbuster, which Icahn called the worst investment he ever made. They listened as I explained how we ran the business differently, were still very profitable, and would soon retire our debt, which for our smaller size, was every bit as daunting as Blockbuster's. But when we ended the meeting, they only seemed angrier and showed no interest in buying the stores out of bankruptcy.

The rest of the meetings with Wall Street bankers were equally unproductive. By now, it seemed no one wanted to have anything to do with Blockbuster. Too much money had already been lost, they said—at which point, I asked why so many had bought Blockbuster's debt in its recent refinancing: $675 million. Their answer provided a rare glimpse into what had been wrong with Blockbuster from the beginning. The company was heavily influenced by too many people with too much money, too much power, and way too much ignorance of what the Blockbuster business was all about. These Wall Street bankers lent Blockbuster $675 million just six months before they filed for bankruptcy. Why? Because they believed that in the event of bankruptcy, they would be made whole from store liquidation sales.

I knew that was not the case and asked the bankers how they had arrived at that conclusion. They handed me a thick book provided by a third party that specialized in conducting liquidation sales. I gave it a quick review and found it short on facts and long on assumptions by people who had no idea what they were talking about. But the bankers believed it; unfortunately for them, they would soon learn the truth.

Over the course of the next several weeks, various reorganization solutions were explored. But somewhere in the process, the *real* liquidation value of the stores was learned, and instead of closing the stores and recovering their $675 million loans, the senior bondholders put the stores on the auction block. The opening bid was set at just $290 million, less than half what they believed them to be worth a few weeks before. Reality had hit the lenders right in the face.

In April 2011, six months after filing bankruptcy, Dish Network Corporation won the auction to buy Blockbuster's assets for $320 million, a shocking decline from the $8.4 billion Viacom paid for the company just 16 years before. Surprisingly, in the year leading to bankruptcy, Blockbuster generated almost $1 billion *more* in sales than in 1994, the year Huizenga sold it to Viacom. But in pursuit of growth at all costs, Blockbuster had opened too many stores and strayed from the fundamentals that made them so successful. Netflix and Redbox understood the business far better and took full advantage.

Blockbuster's bankruptcy left a long trail of carnage. Shareholders, of course, lost everything. Creditors received pennies on the dollar, and subordinated bondholders lost the entire $300 million still owed them. And what about the senior bondholders who, just a few months before, believed they were whole on a $675 million loan? They were paid about $179 million.

The experience of the bankruptcy process taught me a lot about why Blockbuster was the way it was. It had been managed and controlled by people who did not understand the fundamentals of the business and had little curiosity outside their own narrow field of vision.

This theme could be traced all the way back to Wayne Huizenga, who opened over 3,000 Blockbuster stores in just seven years but did not know much about how they worked. Subsequent CEOs had their own distinct way of carrying out their "vision" but missed major shifts in consumer behavior because they lacked an in-depth understanding of the business. Add to that a board of directors that had no firsthand knowledge of the business and which rubber-stamped virtually everything management wanted to do. That was even true of Carl Icahn. Despite all the noise he made before and after he gained control of the board, he went along with management most of the time because he did not know enough about the business to voice a logical argument. His complaints about Blockbuster management were mostly uninformed bluster.

And most recently, Wall Street bankers, who should have known better, lost hundreds of millions of dollars because a supposed expert in video store liquidations entered a bunch of numbers in a spreadsheet that bore no resemblance to reality. It occurred to me that if that liquidation company—or one of the bankers— had made a five-minute phone call to someone who had actually *closed* a Blockbuster store, those hundreds of millions could have been saved for a more productive investment. There was a total disconnect between the people who pulled all the strings and the people who knew what the business was about.

In all my years with Blockbuster, that had been the recurring theme—well-meaning people making critical decisions from 30,000 feet when those decisions could best be made on the ground, in the stores, listening to operators and customers about what *really* happened in a Blockbuster store. But from the company's founding until its very end, that was never a part of Blockbuster's DNA.

In the years leading to bankruptcy, our franchise stores were subjected to untold bad press because of Blockbuster's persistent financial difficulties. We couldn't even have a sale without customers believing it was a "going out of business" sale. For every step forward, it was two steps back due to negative headlines about Blockbuster's mass store closures, layoffs, and eventual bankruptcy. How many thousands of customers left our stores because most of what they heard about Blockbuster was bad? It was a daily battle to convince them we were not going away.

Although we had survived, the Blockbuster ticket no longer stood for the proud brand it once was. More than anything else, it was now a symbol of failure and more a weight around our necks than a benefit. For years, every day had been an uphill battle to protect our stores while Blockbuster was destroying theirs. And now, we had been passed on to a new owner, Charlie Ergen and Dish Network. We had no idea what to expect.

CHAPTER 14

THE FINAL YEARS

"Dish has indicated that they view Blockbuster as a going concern, but our concern is where it's going."

—CRAIG MOFFETT, SANFORD BERNSTEIN ANALYST[66]

Bankruptcy reorganization resulted in a much smaller Blockbuster. Dish closed several hundred unprofitable stores and kept about 1,500 open in the U.S.—one-third the peak of a few years earlier. Franchisees had closed stores at a similar rate, and now there were about 300 left. The only international markets generating meaningful sales were the United Kingdom and Mexico but not enough to impact the company's future one way or the other. The studios had a lien on the 450 stores in Canada and would soon liquidate them, which was a terrible loss given that many of them were still extraordinarily profitable.

In stark contrast, our company was still operating 38 stores in Texas and Alaska. We had closed only three. To reduce overhead, we had laid off three support people in our corporate office in

Austin but, other than that, it was business as usual. Although sales had fallen for three straight years, we were financially strong, which was good since we still had over $2 million in debt to retire.

But uncertainty loomed, especially since bankruptcy law gave Dish the right to reject our franchise agreements. Every remaining franchisee could have been forced to "de-flag," which would have required the removal of the Blockbuster brand and the store computer system. The cost would have been extraordinarily high—perhaps prohibitively so. The next few months were tense as we waited for an answer from Dish. Thankfully, they decided to keep the franchisees and of course, we would continue to pay them for the minimal support they would provide—well over $1 million a year in our case.

Dish planned to expand their satellite television business through their newly acquired chain of retail storefronts—something they never had before. In addition, they would integrate the Blockbuster brand into their Dish satellite offerings. In fact, when Dish bought Blockbuster, Chairman Charlie Ergen said he believed the brand alone was worth the $320 million they'd paid. The stores also offered a retail base from which to launch Dish's long-planned wireless telephone business. That, of course, did not happen, and now 10 years later, Dish is still not in that business.

Not surprisingly, there was much conflict between Dish management and the remaining Blockbuster people. The companies were very different. Dish was founded by Charlie Ergen, who still runs the company today. He has his detractors, but there is no doubt about who was in charge, and the company clearly reflected his no-nonsense, results-oriented style. In contrast, Blockbuster had been through multiple owners and several CEOs. It had struggled for years to define what it stood for. Like them or not, Dish knew exactly who they were, and the cultures of the two companies mixed like oil and water.

Dish had ambitious plans, and certainly, they had the capital to carry them out. Their plans to integrate Dish satellite offerings with stores were smartly conceived and, on paper, looked promising. Mike Ryan, a consultant hired to help develop the store plan, understood the value of pricing power and inventory management. They even had plans to replace the patched-up, archaic store computer system.

Led by Ryan, Dish aggressively tested several pricing strategies, most of which were variations of what had been so successful in our stores for the past 20 years. I got a chuckle when they used my name to label their pricing tests. They called them: 1) The Payne Hybrid, 2) The Pure Payne, and 3) The Aggressive Payne. Each test was intended to maximize the availability of new releases and improve value with lower-priced catalog titles—the same approach that drove more customers to our stores than any in the country.

Ryan and his team were the first Blockbuster managers that took the time to ask the right questions, evaluate the data, and try to understand why our strategy worked. For the last 10 years, our stores had been the most profitable in the entire company. But remarkably, Dish management was the first to try to understand why.

When Dish started to test lower prices, I expressed concern that the store inventories were not adequate to support their strategy. The business was much more than having a few thousand DVDs on the shelves. They had to be the right titles in the right quantities, but years of mismanagement had left the stores with anemic inventories. Then Dish made it worse by getting into no-win negotiations with studios. They were already a huge customer of the studios and believed they could use that leverage to get better deals for DVDs. They even refused to buy several big new releases when they did not get their way. On release day, they would instead send store managers to Walmart and other retailers to buy them. Many retailers refused to sell them large quantities, which resulted in massive out of stocks in stores. Dish had made the inventory problem they inherited even worse, and the death spiral returned.

It became apparent Dish was not committed to sustaining adequate inventory in the stores. Either they did not understand its importance or simply did not want to spend the money to do it right. Sales declines steepened, and they pulled back even more. Then less than a year after Dish had bought the stores and spoken so positively about their plans, it became apparent they were not committed to seeing it through.

The strategy began to fall apart. A little more than a year after Dish had bought the stores, the company started closing them. It became obvious they were throwing in the towel. A year later, only 400 stores remained, and Dish announced that the last would close in January 2014, less than 3 years after they had bought the stores out of bankruptcy. It was a short-lived attempt to preserve a great American brand.

Blockbuster's demise had been an ongoing story for the last 10 years. Its struggles to deal with Netflix, Redbox, and the eventual transition from DVD to digital had been well-chronicled every step of the way. Although there had been a few minor successes, they were mostly superficial attempts to placate Wall Street. The real problems in the stores had never been addressed. For those who understood that, the end had been inevitable for years.

January 2014. Dish had closed the last corporately owned Blockbuster store. What was once a 5,000-store chain of Blockbuster stores in the U.S. was now gone. And of the 1,200 franchised stores, there were only 50 left in the U.S., and 26 of them were ours—13 in Alaska and 13 in Texas. We had been forced to close 15 stores—about a third, but all the remaining stores were profitable. In fact, they were still producing profit margins that were higher than any Blockbuster stores of the last 20 years. But we could not escape the destruction of the Blockbuster brand. Sales were continuing to decline. And now, we were about to be cut off from what was left of our franchisor.

Dish was washing its hands of Blockbuster, and with only 50 franchise stores left, the costs necessary to support those stores could not be justified. So, after announcing they would close all corporately owned Blockbuster stores, Dish informed us that all franchise support services would end. We would be 100 percent on our own.

With this announcement, Dish had defaulted on its franchise agreements. Although they were contractually obligated to maintain essential services, Dish was pulling out. Franchisees could either sue Dish for damages or work out a reasonable solution to keep stores operating. Border Entertainment was still a viable business with several hundred employees, so it was critical we find an answer.

Dish did not want legal conflict any more than we did, and we quickly reached an amicable solution. Instead of paying up to 10 percent of total sales in royalties and other fees, as had been the case for the past 20 years, Dish agreed to a 2 percent "licensing" fee for the use of the Blockbuster brand, which they still own. It was a fair deal and avoided needless litigation.

The discontinued franchise services did not amount to much. For the last several years, franchisees had been essentially on their own. Blockbuster had done more to hurt our stores than help. However, there was one service we had to have—the store computer system. As archaic as it was, it was all we had. And without support from Dish, we did not know if it would continue to function. For years, most essential maintenance and support had been done centrally, by "computer support." We couldn't even collect data directly from the stores. It had to be requested from Blockbuster, which retrieved it daily. What's worse, routine maintenance of prices, products, and promotions could not be done in the stores. It had to be "coded" by computer support and downloaded. The system was never intended to be maintained by the stores and required knowledgeable computer systems people for routine maintenance and troubleshooting.

After a brief period of panic, a long-time computer support manager at Blockbuster came to the rescue. Dave Carrera's first job with Blockbuster was in 1992 as a "Customer Service Representative" in one of Blockbuster's first stores in Dallas. Although he had no formal computer training, he was recruited to computer support in 1995 to bolster the department's store expertise and had been there ever since. He had held multiple positions and was one of the few survivors of multiple layoffs, bankruptcy, and eventually, Dish.

Dave knew more about the computer system than anyone, and thankfully, he wanted to help the remaining franchisees survive. He developed a way to keep the stores running when disconnected from corporate and developed the procedures necessary to maintain it. We were forced to give up a lot of reporting systems we had relied on for years, but Dave's system addressed all the essentials needed to keep the stores running. It was complicated and required a rework of the communication infrastructure in every store to handle credit card transactions and the transmission of essential data.

Dave essentially became our computer support department out of his home in Plano, Texas, and signed on as a consultant. He kept the store computer systems running smoothly until we closed the last store. When stores needed help—which was often—Dave was always there. Without him, our survival for the next four years would not have been possible.

With Dave on board and the computer issues resolved, we settled into managing the business. Everything was stacked against us, but we still had over 100,000 customers visiting our stores every month, and several hundred loyal employees led by managers who were as committed as ever. We had a strategy we believed in, and everyone was determined to keep the stores running as long as possible.

Looking back, we all believe we did some of our best work during those challenging times. As we continued to downsize, everyone took on additional responsibilities. Eventually, our corporate support staff was downsized from 13 to 2, me and the company controller Barbara Talbot, who assumed all the accounting and administrative responsibilities. We both worked out of our homes during the last few years.

We had retired our debt two years before Dish threw in the towel, which gave us much needed financial flexibility. This helped us maintain our commitment to compete with Netflix by maintaining massive inventories and with Redbox by having the best availability of new releases. We never wavered from this strategy, and in fact, strengthened it in those final years as studios reduced prices for DVDs.

Within a couple of years after Dish cut us loose, all the franchise stores had closed except ours, and the one you have probably heard about in Bend, Oregon. But even though we had lasted the longest, the carnage left by Blockbuster's demise was an ongoing challenge. Market forces were working against us, and the tarnished Blockbuster brand was universally regarded as the big loser in the home entertainment business.

The ongoing decline also meant we could no longer commit to long-term leases, and as they expired, we attempted to negotiate short-term extensions. Several landlords cooperated, but others did not, and we were forced to close still profitable stores before their time. As landlords soon discovered, those 5,000 square foot buildings were difficult to lease, and many sat idle for years after we closed. Some are still vacant today.

Over the next 4 years, we continued to close stores—a few each year. With each closing, the attention from the media became more intense. We were the last chain of Blockbuster stores in the U.S. and were gradually going away. Our story was told on multiple national media outlets. Most of the nation's Blockbusters had been gone for years, and with them, the great memories of going to the stores with friends and family. It seemed everyone wanted to know how we were still in business and what it was like.

I turned down more interviews than I agreed to, even an opportunity to be featured on the Jimmy Kimmel show. We were extremely proud of how long we had lasted and how we did it against long odds. But telling the story of the last Blockbuster stores was difficult. We did not like closing our final stores and did not think we would have been doing so had it not been for years of reckless mismanagement by Blockbuster executives, many of whom had "made theirs" and moved on. For years, it had been "us against the world," and now it was coming to an end. There were a lot of great memories, but it was difficult to accept what we all believed was a premature outcome.

Most media were looking for sound bites about how we lasted so long and "feel-good" stories about the "good old days." But the story was much too complex for sound bites, which is one of many reasons I chose to write this book. And although time has helped us all feel better about the final years, we were not all smiles during those last closures. There were a lot of raw emotions that have taken time to put in perspective.

We closed the last stores in El Paso in 2016—23 years after opening the first and more than 10 years after Blockbuster's financial decline began. The closing sales in the last 4 stores began on the same day. Prior to opening the doors, over a hundred customers lined up outside each store, and once inside, many waited over 2 hours to check out, some buying a hundred or more DVDs. All the final closing sales were organized chaos. The fire department even showed up at one and had us close the doors because the size of the crowd had become unsafe.

El Paso was a city of about 550,000 people and had always been our most competitive market. Quality sites for stores were abundant and inexpensive compared to other large markets. Hollywood Video took full advantage and opened 10 stores in just a few years in the mid-1990s. For the next several years, it was "our ten versus their ten." Twenty video superstores in a city of 550,000 was unprecedented and made it the most competitive market of its size in the country.

Hollywood's entry slashed our profit by more than half, the same as it had done to Blockbuster stores all over the country. But under the direction of Alex Marin, who ran those stores for many years, we successfully fought back, and soon the stores were more profitable than ever. It was a remarkable accomplishment; one Blockbuster could have learned from but did not.

We honed our competitive skills in El Paso and used much of what we learned there in our other markets. What worked there worked everywhere—even in the absence of stiff competition. Our partner in the development of all those strategies was our long-time advertising agency, Mithoff Burton Partners. They were based in El Paso but managed our advertising in all our stores, including Alaska. For years, we would bring them rough ideas of what we wanted to do, and their team would create the message and the best means to communicate it. They developed countless slogans and talking points that helped position our stores as the ones with the most movies and the best prices, the core strategy of everything we did—the story of *abundance*.

Because Blockbuster's strategies differed so drastically from ours, we had to build our own image, and our advertising message often conflicted with theirs. It was a constant battle, and I have often wondered how successful we all could have been had we joined forces rather than constantly fought each other in the media.

Bill Burton, Chana Burton, Peter Fraire, and many others at Mithoff Burton did a remarkable job helping us compete on our own terms. As DVD grew, Walmart, the largest retailer in the world, became a direct competitor. To answer the new challenge, Bill and his team developed the "El Paso's DVD Collection" theme to explain there was no need to invest in a home video library. Our Blockbuster stores already had all of them—and most of it rented for $.99! We even produced our own television commercials with customers bragging about how they kept their personal DVD collection at Blockbuster and were willing to "share it." It was genius, and it worked beautifully.

Then Netflix by-mail totally changed the game. We were fighting a competitor we couldn't see. I told Bill we had to position our stores as "having everything." If Netflix had it, we had to have it, too. That led to some of the best marketing we ever did. Bill and his team developed "We've Got It, Or We'll Get It" and designed the advertising that literally screamed the message in our markets. *Every* store had *every* DVD a customer had ever asked for! And the advertising message continued to remind them.

Perhaps, more than anything else, those two messages and the relentless execution of them in the stores kept our company strong as Blockbuster deteriorated. Still, today, I wonder about the outcome if Blockbuster had adopted "America's DVD Collection" as their theme and purpose. Almost 6,000 stores, one within 15 minutes of 90 percent of American homes, telling everyone there was no need to spend their money buying DVDs. Blockbuster already had them all—and you could rent them for a fraction of the price of buying them.

The same went for Netflix. Why pay a monthly fee when you can pay as you go for less and get any movie you want—*when* you want it? It was a powerful message and capitalized on the *strengths* of the stores instead of weakening them by recklessly pursuing misguided strategies. Instead of more for less, Blockbuster CEOs had, for years, consistently pursued strategies that resulted in fewer movies for rent—at higher prices! It was in direct contradiction to everything customers wanted, which had been made so obvious by Netflix and Redbox.

As the business declined, we eventually ceased most advertising and discontinued our day-to-day relationship with Mithoff Burton. Then, when the final El Paso stores closed in 2016, it was like cutting out part of our soul. That ultra-competitive market had been difficult, but in partnership with Bill and his team, we had answered every challenge. Our longevity was evidence that we got most things right. If only Blockbuster had joined us!

In early 2018, we closed our last store in Texas, which was located in Edinburg. Because it was the last Blockbuster in Texas, the state where the first store had opened in Dallas 33 years before, the story attracted national press coverage. The closure was especially emotional for Rick and Liz Cavazos, the managers of the store. They met working at Blockbuster in 1999 and were married a year later. Their daughter began working at the store in 2017 and was still there when it closed.

About a year earlier, Liz had helped close a store when a story emerged that illustrated how much our stores meant to so many people. An autistic child had been a regular customer of that store. His parents were crushed when they learned the store would close; they were worried about how their child would react because trips to Blockbuster had become such a comforting routine. So, Liz worked with the parents to create a "mini Blockbuster store" in their home. She gave them a few fixtures and a couple hundred movies to display on them—movies she knew the child liked and had rented over and over. The story went viral and was run by media all over the country. It remains one of the most touching events from those days of closing the final stores.

A few weeks later, we made the final decision to close the last two stores in Alaska, one in Anchorage and the other in Fairbanks. By now, the attention from the media had intensified even more. The most surprising came from the John Oliver Show on HBO called "Last Week Tonight." They had heard about the "last Blockbuster stores in Alaska," and decided they would help us stay open with a new attraction. They had spent several thousand dollars acquiring movie memorabilia owned by actor Russell Crowe, which included the trunks, robe, and groin protector he wore in the boxing movie *Cinderella Man*, as well as wardrobe items from *Les Misérables* and *Robin Hood*. After having some fun with it on the show, Oliver announced he was giving all of it to us to display in our last Anchorage store! The idea was to give people a new reason to visit one of the last Blockbuster stores. Maybe it would help us stay open longer.

I explained to the producer of the show that we had already made plans to close and, although we were very grateful, we did not expect the memorabilia to save it. That did not deter them, and they shipped it to us anyway, complete with beautiful glass cabinets for display. Later, we gave the groin protector back to them for a subsequent comedy bit, but we still own the rest. It is now on permanent loan to the very last Blockbuster store in Bend, Oregon, and will be there until it closes—although owner Ken Tisher has no plans to do so. In a truly serendipitous moment, Ron Howard, who directed *Cinderella Man*, visited the store and took a selfie in front of the boxing robe. He posted the photo on his Facebook page with the comment: "I indulged in a trip down my cinematic memory lane."

The last Blockbuster stores in Alaska closed in August 2018. I made my final business trip to Alaska a couple of weeks before they closed for good to say my final good-byes to Kevin Daymude and Kelli Vey, the last managers, and to the rest of the store staffs. Kevin and Kelli had both been with the company for 30 years and were our longest-tenured employees. How fitting it was to have them close our last 2 stores. Throughout the closures of all our stores, which took place over a six-year period, not one employee left until the job was done. It was a tribute to the leadership qualities of Kevin, Kelli, and all the great managers who led our stores over the course of 30 years.

It was my last business trip to visit stores, and I kept my emotions in check until I went to the Anchorage airport to leave for the last time. For three decades, that airport had been the gateway to our stores. One does not *drive* to most places in Alaska, certainly not cities like Kodiak and Juneau. There are no roads. And the roads to cities like Fairbanks, Soldotna, and Kenai are long and often closed by bad weather. I had made countless trips through the Anchorage airport to all those cities, most of them accompanied by Craig Cobb, who so successfully ran the Alaska operation for over 20 years. We had spent countless hours in the Anchorage airport, as well as all the others around the state, wondering if the weather would allow us to fly, which it often did not. How many times had we made the "milk run" to Ketchikan, which was a 5-hour 1,500-mile flight with 3 stops along the way? And we will never forget the pilot in Kodiak walking on the wings with a broom, trying to sweep enough snow off the plane so we could take off. The great memories, along with the frustrations of flying in Alaska, were endless.

So, when I took a seat in the Anchorage International Airport to await my last flight home from Alaska, the emotions came pouring out. I called my wife sobbing, trying to understand what had just hit me. This airport carried memories of flights in and out of this city, where almost two-thirds of the people of Alaska live. I had spent countless days and nights traveling to our stores throughout the state. Every trip still carried memories of all the employees and outside partners who worked with us to build what, by any measure, was the most successful chain of Block-buster stores in the U.S. For me, it had been 25 years of fulfilling a dream—building a company, building a team, making our own decisions. And exceeding all expectations.

Our stores had provided the first job for thousands of people over the course of almost 30 years. And it was a training ground for ambitious employees to become managers and learn how to run a business. How to hire and train great employees. How to merchandise stores. How to manage costs and understand an income statement. And most important, how to build teams of people who understood and bought into common goals. Those teams of people built the longest lasting chain of Blockbuster stores in the country. It always seemed more like a mission than work.

And with that last flight out of Anchorage, it was over.

CONCLUSION

During three years of research and writing, I was asked many times: "Why are you writing this book?" I usually answered with another question: "If we can't learn something from the story of Blockbuster, what's the point?" How can a company as dominant as Blockbuster fail so spectacularly, years before digital entertainment was a factor? We need to know why.

This book has been a personal journey to find the answers, and the experience has been both satisfying and frustrating. *Satisfying* because I was able to "connect the dots" and better understand what happened. But *frustrating* because it became evident that most of Blockbuster's problems were self-inflicted.

The genesis of virtually all of Blockbuster's difficulties came from its lack of intellectual curiosity, the ultimate example of which was the inept mismanagement of its massive movie viewing database. They never developed this goldmine of information that would have given them an incomparable base of knowledge with which to lead, instead of always following. When being biggest was not enough, Blockbuster lacked the business intelligence to know what to do next.

Instead of relentlessly pursuing fact-based solutions, complacency dominated. The result was a wanton ignorance that left Blockbuster defenseless against anyone who better understood why people watched movies. Reed Hastings could not have known it at the time, but when he tried to sell Netflix to Blockbuster in 2000, his company already had a doctorate degree in movie knowledge as compared to Blockbuster—which never got past the first grade. Netflix could not beat Blockbuster with money, but they easily did it with a deep understanding of their customers' behavior. Redbox did the same.

Business psychologists have various terms for such behavior, but I like Bill Gates' simple observation. *"Success is a lousy teacher. It seduces smart people into thinking they can't lose."* Blockbuster was the embodiment of this characterization. Overwhelming success in its early years created unwarranted contentment that became permanently embedded in its culture. This led to repeated attempts to solve complicated problems with superficial solutions.

Now, more than a decade after Blockbuster filed bankruptcy, the story still resonates. It was an iconic brand—a company that seemed to have it all. But today, *all* that remains is the consummate example of a company that was *built to fail*.

I am indebted to all the people from Blockbuster's past who told me their story. I am especially thankful to Jim Keyes, Nick Shepherd, Shane Evangelist, and Nigel Travis for the time they gave me. They were all open and candid about their experiences at Blockbuster. They will not agree with many of my conclusions, but we will have to agree to disagree. With the benefit of hindsight, I hope we can all look back on the story of Blockbuster and be honest and objective about what happened. That is the only way we can learn from it.

I had hoped John Antioco would discuss how he chose to manage Blockbuster through the most transformative period in its history. To the best of my knowledge, he has never publicly addressed these issues in detail. Except to attribute Blockbuster's failure to others, he has been mostly an onlooker as its demise is incessantly dissected.

Although Antioco and I talked, he declined to answer questions. He only reiterated his belief that had his plans been carried out by his successors, Blockbuster would today be a major player in digital entertainment distribution. But saying it does not make it so. Netflix began streaming movies the year Antioco left, but Blockbuster had no plans nor the resources to launch a competing service.

Of all the former Blockbuster executives I contacted about this book, Antioco is the only one who would not answer questions. As has been the case since his early days at Blockbuster, most of Antioco's communication has been one-way and from a safe distance.

I have read a lot of business books in my day and greatly admire writers like Jim Collins, who has written several books about why some companies succeed, and others fail. Like most great business writers, he has a way of studying the behavior of companies and then conceptualizing it, so the lessons learned can be applied to other businesses.

Collins' most recent book, *How the Mighty Fall*, describes five common steps to failure and reads like he was sitting in Blockbuster's boardroom dissecting their every move. Step one was "Hubris Born of Success," which perfectly describes Blockbuster's state of mind when I became a franchisee in 1993, and the subsequent four steps perfectly describe what I observed during the company's march to failure.

So, how *did* Netflix and Redbox seize the day instead of Blockbuster? What concepts and business practices resulted in that outcome instead of Blockbuster maintaining its rightful place as the king of home entertainment? I hope this book answered a lot of those questions. But are there *concepts* that can be applied to other businesses? Most certainly, and even though I am not a professional business writer, I am going to attempt to play one and describe what I learned from my 25 years as a Blockbuster franchisee. And since most of those business writers seem to prefer the number "7," here are my:

SEVEN LESSONS FROM THE STORY OF BLOCKBUSTER

1. *Clearly define your company's purpose—its mission.* For years, over half of American households visited a video store every week. The freedom to watch any movie at any time was a revolution that began in the 1980s and continued into the new millennium. By opening more stores than anyone else, Blockbuster led the way and became a fixture of American culture. That should have been celebrated and led to a clearly defined mission for how Blockbuster would develop its role as the largest provider of movies of any business in the country—more than all theaters combined. But despite its dominance, Blockbuster never clearly defined what it was about, and the mission changed from year to year. There were innocuous mission statements like *"to be the complete source for movies and games."* But *exactly* what did that mean, and how did they intend to get there? The answer often depended on what Wall Street wanted to hear instead of adherence to a clearly defined purpose for being.

2. *Specifically, identify what drives your business and pursue it—relentlessly.* As compared to other retail businesses, video rental was relatively simple, especially as compared to the grocery business, where I learned it. It was always about having the *right movies* at the *right price* in *convenient locations*. It was not rocket science, but not once in the history of Blockbuster did it fully commit to being the best at any of those key drivers. Its systems to identify the right movies were archaic at best. Prices were determined more by short-term sales goals than by careful study of optimal price points. And convenience was compromised by hundreds of stores that were not relocated as retail traffic patterns changed.

3. *Measure What Matters.* Blockbuster's problems began with never clearly defining *what* mattered. So, it is no surprise that what got measured changed from quarter to quarter, sometimes month to month. The goalposts were constantly moved to justify strategy instead of the other way around.

4. *Respect and Learn from Competitors.* This is obvious to anyone who has ever been in a competitive retail business, but it was never a part of Blockbuster's DNA. The company never acted like it even *had* competition until forced to, and then it was too late. It began with a lack of respect for anyone who was not part of the "blue and gold." Because Blockbuster dominated through sheer size, there was broad agreement throughout the company that, "They got it right, and everyone else got it wrong." Therefore, to them, there was no reason to pay attention to anyone else. Perhaps more than any other behavior, this led to Blockbuster's premature downfall.

5. *If you are going to do it—be the BEST.* Other than open more stores than everyone else, Blockbuster never committed to being the best at anything, which is most clearly illustrated by its answer to Netflix. When Blockbuster decided to launch a DVD-by-mail business, management never committed to being the best. The service was underfunded and never approached the industry standards set by Netflix. Blockbuster seemed content to just be *in* the business instead of being the best. This led to flawed strategies to patch up fundamental weaknesses—like giving away millions of free rentals through its Total Access program that it couldn't afford.

6. *In difficult times, rely on fundamentals to survive.* Blockbuster was like a football team at the opponent's goal line that runs a trick play on fourth and inches. If it works, the coach looks like a genius. If it does not, everyone wonders why he did not stick with the fundamentals that got the team there in the first place. Blockbuster never *defined* the fundamentals, so when challenges came, they relied on trick plays instead. None of them worked, and in most cases, they made the situation worse.

7. *Don't just talk about the future. PLAN for it.* In its early days, Wayne Huizenga talked about how Blockbuster would transition to whatever came next in home entertainment. Every subsequent CEO said the same. But none invested sufficient capital or brainpower to be ready when the time came. Instead of leading, Blockbuster was always content to be a bystander while innovators defined the future.

Maybe I should have added an eighth. "Have Fun!" It rarely seemed like Blockbuster was having fun. They had their share of great parties, especially in the early days. But it never felt like they considered the business of running video stores fun. At Border Entertainment, we always had fun, which was often in the form of friendly competition among stores. I believe that drove a passion for the business that helped us discover real solutions to problems when others did not.

But passion for a business must be guided by principle. So, I want to close this book with the business principles that guided everything we did at Border Entertainment. They were posted in prominent places in all our stores so employees, as well as customers, could see them. These principles were a product of our passion for the business and our constant desire to be the absolute best we could be. I hope you will find some principles you can apply to *your* business.

PRINCIPLES OF BUSINESS CONDUCT

BORDER ENTERTAINMENT is a small company that is a BIG provider of entertainment. When people in our communities watch movies, more choose our Blockbuster stores than any other source—including theaters. The company's owners are committed to the following Principles of Business Conduct as they relate to our Customers, Employees, Communities, and Competitors.

Our Customers:

- We provide a store experience that is worthy of our customers' **loyalty** by following fair and easy-to-understand business practices.
- We deliver **outstanding value** by providing convenient locations, attentive customer service, maximum product availability, and lower prices than our primary competitors.
- We deliver an **exceptional customer experience** that meets or exceeds that of any retailer (not just video stores) in the communities we serve.
- **Late fees** are a necessary component of managing product availability for customers. However, they must be managed to minimize customer dissatisfaction.

Our Employees:

- We treat all employees with **respect, dignity**, and **fairness**.
- We create a business environment in which every employee has the opportunity to **learn, excel, be themselves, have fun, and help make Border Entertainment a better place to work and shop.**
- We provide **meaningful employment and career opportunities** commensurate with each employee's abilities and aspirations.
- We offer **exceptional compensation and financial security** to our management team.

Our Communities:

- We are a meaningful component of the economy and the culture of each community we serve. We are committed to making each a better place to live and work by meaningfully contributing our time and money.

Our Competitors:

- We provide an overall movie and game rental experience that **cannot be matched or improved** upon by competitors.
- We continually monitor our competitors and **always know more about them than they know about us.**
- We run our business so well competitors **accept defeat as an unavoidable result.**

My business philosophy has been heavily influenced by great leaders like Charles Butt, who built a regional grocery chain—

H-E-B—into what many believe is the best retail company in the world. And by my all-time business hero, Herb Kelleher, whose unconventional ideas re-defined air travel and built Southwest Airlines into the most valuable—and loved—airline company in the U.S.

But as great as they are—and others like them—they cannot define our own individual paths. We can, and *should*, learn how they challenged conventional wisdom to achieve phenomenal success.

But I believe the most valuable lessons they taught us are to define: our own path, our own purpose, how we will get there, and how we will measure our progress.

No one can do that for us. Every organization has unique challenges that require original ideas, and those can only come from within by following our passion, guided by facts, to the right answers.

ACKNOWLEDGMENTS

I began thinking about this book over three years ago as we were closing our last Blockbuster stores. It began with informal discussions among family members, business associates, and friends. Everyone encouraged me to do it, and I needed it because I wondered if anyone would want to read the story of a company that failed over ten years ago. But in time, it became clear there was still an emotional attachment to Blockbuster, and people really did miss it. Everyone wanted to know what happened. I began to believe the story needed to be told, and because I had been there the longest, I was in the best position to tell it.

Early support came from my son, Tyler, and my daughter, Kelsey. When they said, "Dad, you've got to do this," that was about all the encouragement I needed. My wife, Lyndsay, did not only encourage me, she was a part of the process from beginning to end. She patiently listened to me read every word in this book—more than once—and helped me think through every story and lesson to be learned. When I couldn't get through the final chapter without breaking down, I handed the manuscript to her so she could read it to me. Having lived the entire Blockbuster story with me, she fought back the tears, too, but got through it. Without the total support of my family, this book could not have been written.

Thank you to Tucker Max, the founder of Scribe Media, J.T. McCormick, its President and CEO, and Hal Clifford, its Editor-In-Chief. They built their company to help nonwriters like me tell important stories that might not otherwise be told. A special thanks to the team assigned to me, especially Tashan Mehta, who edited my book. Everyone at Scribe is a patient professional, and this book would not have been possible without their guidance.

I spent days on the phone with Scott Watson, Blockbuster's first international franchisee, and Founder and President of the Association of Blockbuster Franchisees (ABF). More than anyone else, he helped me identify and think through the parts of the story that most needed to be told. And he was an essential part of the research process, helping pull together notes and minutes from ABF Board meetings, and supplying me with a truckload of old business periodicals from pre-internet years that were not available online.

Thank you to my franchise friends who joined in our reminiscing dinner in Memphis to help make sure I got the story right. Enjoying a fine dinner that night were Scott Watson, Fred Montesi, Bob Wenner, Tom Barzizza, Jody Brown, and Keith Cole. Several great stories in the book came from that dinner.

Thank you to fellow franchisee Mitch Kerns, who helped piece together the story of how Blockbuster decided to end late fees.

It began over lunch with John Antioco but ended with the rollout of a program that was nothing like what had worked in his stores, and which hastened Blockbuster's descent to failure.

To Charles Butt and everyone at H-E-B. They may be the best retailer in the world, but they will never act like it, which is why they will always be the best. The foundation of everything I learned about business was built in my fifteen years with that company. My sympathies to anyone who tries to compete with them.

To Craig Odanovich, Greg Smith, Roger Davidson, and the entire team at Video Central. We built something that was more special than you will ever know. Everything we did in our Blockbuster stores at Border Entertainment came from what we started at Video Central. We had an exceptional team that, unfortunately, never got to fulfill its potential.

Thank you to Alan Markert, a past Vice President at H-E-B, who helped recreate the detail of Blockbuster's missed opportunity to buy H-E-B's Video Central stores and their subsequent sell to Hollywood Video. That story is perhaps as important as Blockbuster's pass on buying Netflix seven years later, but it has never previously been told.

To Bill Wildman at Pinnacle Capital. He was the driving force behind the $13 million loan that started Border Entertainment. He taught me all about leverage and how to use debt to build a business. Our company would have never existed without what I learned from Bill.

To Wil Stevens who cleared hurdle after hurdle to secure the equity investment in Border Entertainment. Along with Bill Wildman, they were the angels that made sure the deal got done. They opened their mind and their hearts to what we were all about and were about the only ones who "got it."

Thank you to all my friends and associates at Blockbuster. We did not agree on much, and I wish the outcome had been different. But it was never personal. We agreed to disagree and pressed on. Thank you for your professionalism.

Jim Keyes gave me many hours of his time to tell the story of Blockbuster's final years. The surprise revelation of all those conversations was Blockbuster having to turn down the opportunity to buy the digital content rights for Starz and Epix, which Netflix later bought to jump-start their streaming business. Because of nondisclosure agreements, that story had never been told, but Keyes obtained permission to tell it. A special thank you to Jim Keyes for a story that is the ultimate example of a "fork in the road" that changed the course of entertainment history.

Thank you to Greg Meyer, the founder of DVDXpress, who told the story about the beginning of his DVD kiosk business in New York City, his attempts to partner with Blockbuster, and of course, that haunting story of 9/11.

We had a lot of partners outside the company who helped, but most important was Curt Nading, a real estate developer in Alaska whom I met in 1993. We formed an enduring partnership that produced some of the best Blockbuster stores in the world. He was one of the few developers who understood we were every bit as strong as national tenants and consistently gave us first shot at some of the best locations in the state.

We could have never come close to reaching our full potential without our relationship with Mithoff Burton Partners, our advertising agency in El Paso, Texas. They took the time to understand what we needed, then put the full force of their team behind us. They helped get our messaging right, which was often in direct conflict with what Blockbuster was pushing on the national stage. It was always an uphill battle, but they persevered to the very end. I am eternally grateful to Bill Burton, Chana Burton, Peter Fraire, and the entire team at Mithoff Burton Partners for the great work they did for us.

Thank you to Tim Shanahan and Tom Kielty at Video Products Distributors (VPD). They built an outstanding company that was our primary supplier for over 20 years and the ultimate example of what a business partner should be.

To Don Jeffries, retired Executive Vice President of 20th Century Fox Home Entertainment. Under Don's leadership, Fox formed an enduring partnership with our company as well as the entire Blockbuster franchise community. And in preparation for this book, he was my "go-to" to help me better understand the Blockbuster story from the perspective of the Hollywood studios.

Thank you to Dave Carrera, who came to the rescue when we thought we might not have a computer system to run the stores when Dish ceased support. The last four years would not have been possible without his expertise.

And thank you to everyone who was ever a part of the team at

Border Entertainment. There were thousands, and you all helped build an exceptional company we can all be proud of. Thank you to Bob Beerman, our CFO, who so skillfully managed our cash, our bankers, and our equity partners. To Barbara Talbot, our Controller, who was the true force in our general office for the entire life of Border and the very last employee to leave—after she made sure everything had been properly wrapped up. To Mark Merriam, who managed all our purchasing. He was the brains behind the most important part of our business—the management of all the product.

Craig Cobb was the ultimate retail professional and built a phenomenal organization in Alaska. Our seventeen Blockbuster stores in that state were some of the most successful in the world, and except for Ken Tisher's store in Bend, Oregon, the very last to close. When Craig left a few years before we closed the last stores, Kevin Daymude and Kelli Vey, our longest-tenured employees, expertly managed the final stores until they closed the last ones in August 2018. Alaska was a special place to run a business and we had special people to lead us.

El Paso was an exceptionally competitive market that had more video superstores than any city of its size in the country, but Alex Marin built an organization that met every challenge. He was exceptionally driven and always faced challenges head on, both attributes that were necessary to succeed in such a highly competitive market.

In 2006, when we bought the stores in the Rio Grande Valley of Texas, they were close to failure. But Roland Deleon totally bought into our plan and successfully steered the stores back to profitability. The same was true with the 25 stores we helped Glenn Klicker manage in the southeast. Both showed that failing stores could be brought back from the dead if they gave customers what they wanted. Unfortunately, Blockbuster was not watching.

And thank you to Rick and Liz Cavazos, who closed our final few stores in Texas, the state where the Blockbuster story began. They were loyal to the end and finished the job with pure class.

I have saved my last thank you for someone I never knew, Herb Kelleher. He started Southwest Airlines in 1967, and I followed their story every step of the way, from the hot pants and free drinks days of the 1970s to being deemed the airline most likely to survive Covid 19 in 2020. When Herb died in January 2019, I felt like I lost a mentor. He was my business hero. Herb had a unique view of what air travel should be, and it was nothing like what others envisioned. His approach to the business was radical to many, and he faced obstacles and challenges most would have succumbed to. But he never gave in and built Southwest from "the little airline that could" into the most valuable airline in the country.

Herb was my inspiration because he demonstrated that the conventional way is not necessarily the best way. Watching Herb run Southwest Airlines helped give me the freedom to think for myself, challenge convention, and find my own answers. Almost everything he did came from an original idea, and in most cases, it was the *right* idea. When Herb died, the employees of Southwest Airlines gave him the ultimate tribute with their own original idea. They paid for a national television spot to thank Herb Kelleher for everything he had done for them. It was the ultimate send-off for the most original business thinker I ever knew.

As Herb Kelleher did for me, I hope this book has helped free your mind from convention, which is often stuck in tired ideas from the past. Allow your passion, guided by facts, to lead you to the right answers.

NOTES

1   Roston, Tom 2017, *I Lost It at the Video Store*, 117

2   Apar, Bruce, "Spielberg Meets Lou Berg," *Video Business*, August 18, 1989.

3   Stewart, James B., 2006, *Disney War*, Simon & Schuster, 93.

4   Roston, Tom 2017, *I Lost It at the Video Store*, 64.

5   DeGeorge, Gail, 1996, *The Making of a Blockbuster*, John Wiley & Sons, 59.

6   DeGeorge, Gail, 1996, *The Making of a Blockbuster*, John Wiley & Sons, 58.

7   DeGeorge, Gail, 1996, *The Making of a Blockbuster*, John Wiley & Sons, 101.

8   Hyatt, Joshua, *He Began Blockbuster. So What?* July 1, 2003, money.cnn.com/magazines.

9   DeGeorge, Gail, 1996, *The Making of a Blockbuster*, John Wiley & Sons, 58.

10 Desjardins, Doug, "Blockbuster Creator David Cook Recalls Events That Launched Chain," *Video Store*, November 12, 1995.

11 DeGeorge, Gail, 1996, *The Making of a Blockbuster*, John Wiley & Sons, 100.

12 DeGeorge, Gail, 1996, *The Making of a Blockbuster*, John Wiley & Sons, 116.

13 DeGeorge, Gail, 1996, *The Making of a Blockbuster,* John Wiley & Sons, 130.

14 DeGeorge, Gail, 1996, *The Making of a Blockbuster,* John Wiley & Sons, 135.

15 Bates, James, "Wayne's World: Blockbuster's Huizenga Dominates Video Rentals, but Technology Threatens to Erase His Lead, *Los Angeles Times*, June 6, 1993.

16 Wickstrom, Andy "Blockbuster Vows to Change Music Retailing," *Video Business*, November 6, 1992.

17 Seigal, Buddy, "Spotlight On Blockbuster," *Video Store*, November 11-15, 1995.

18 Shapiro, Eben, "Synergies Proved Illusory In Viacom-Blockbuster Deal," *Wall Street Journal*, February 21, 1997.

19 Redstone, Sumner, 2001, *A Passion to Win*, Simon & Schuster, 23.

20 Altaner, David, and Fins, Antonio, "Blockbuster in Turmoil," *South Florida Sun Sentinel*, April 27, 1997.

21 Travis, Nigel, 2018, *The Culture Challenge,* Hatchette Book Group, 50.

22 Redstone, Sumner, 2001, *A Passion to Win*, Simon & Schuster, 26-27.

23 Scala, Betsy, "IPO Shines Light on Blockbuster's Losses," *Video Business*, May 17, 1999.

24 Redstone, Sumner, 2001, *A Passion to Win*, Simon & Schuster, 29-30.

25 Travis, Nigel, 2018, *The Culture Challenge,* PublicAffairs Hatchette Book Group, 52.

26 Redstone, Sumner, 2001 *A Passion to Win*, Simon & Schuster, 281.

27 Potter, Charlie, "Nick Saban Pays His Respects to the late Wayne Huizenga," 247sports.com/college/alabama, March 28, 2018.

28 Satell, Greg, "It's Not Enough to Drive Change, You Also Have to Survive Victory," Digitaltonto.com, March 3, 2019.

29 Randolph, Marc, 2019, *That Will Never Work,* Little, Brown and Company, 98.

30 Anderson Forest, Stephanie, "Blockbuster's Fired Up Mr. Fixit," Bloomberg.com/news/articles, February 8, 1998.

31 Ibid.

32 Ibid.

33 "Redstone: We've Changed This Industry," *Video Business,* April 6, 1998.

34 Redstone, Sumner, 2001, *A Passion to Win*, Simon & Schuster, 284.

35 Sweeting, Paul and Netherby, Jennifer, "Studios: Indies Passed on Deals," *Video Business*, June 24, 2002.

36 Ibid.

37 Fabrikant, Geraldine, "Attack of the Disruptive Disk; Sales of DVD's are Challenging the Business of Renting Movies," *New York Times*, April 16, 2001.

38 Fabrikant, Geraldine, "Attack of the Disruptive Disk; Sales of DVD's are Challenging the Business of Renting Movies," *New York Times*, April 16, 2001.

39 Sweeting, Paul, "Forecast: A Big Blue Haze," *Video Business*, December 23, 2002.

40 Sweeting, Paul, "Blockbuster Bolts Out," *Video Business*, April 28, 2003.

41 Anderson,Chris, 2006. *The Long Tail,* Hyperion, 109.

42 Randolph, Marc, 2019, *That Will Never Work*, Little, Brown and Company, 205.

43 Randolph, Marc, 2019, *That Will Never Work*, Little, Brown and Company, 250.

44 Randolph, Marc, 2019, *That Will Never Work*, Little, Brown and Company, 252.

45 Randolph, Marc, 2019, *That Will Never Work*, Little, Brown and Company, 253.

46 Randolph, Marc, 2019, *That Will Never Work*, Little, Brown and Company, 223.

47 Sweeting, Paul, "Blockbuster Likely to Have a Huge Hangover," *Video Business*, February 16, 2004.

48 Sweeting, Paul, "Blockbuster Takes Subscriptions National," *Video Business*, May 31, 2004.

49 "Land of the Giants: The Netflix Effect, Who Really Killed Blockbuster Video?" *podcasts.apple.com*, June 30, 2020.

50 Sweeting, Paul, "Big Blue Plans Double-Barreled Approach to Subs," *Video Business*, April 26, 2004.

51 Cauthen, Shawn, Director, Keating, Gina, Writer, *Netflix vs. the World*, Documentary Film, 2019.

52 Randolph, Marc, 2019, *That Will Never Work*, Little, Brown and Company, 46.

53 Randolph, Marc, 2019, *That Will Never Work*, Little, Brown and Company, 302.

54 Keating, Gina, 2013, *Netflixed: The Epic Battle for America's Eyeballs*, Portfolio/Penguin, 236, "Nick Shepherd, who was Lowe's contact at Blockbuster, does not recall this offer from Lowe but does acknowledge later conversations with Redbox about a joint venture that never happened. See: Keating, Gina, 2013, *Netflixed: The Epic Battle for America's Eyeballs*, Portfolio/Penguin, 236."

55 Strahlberg, David, "Antioco Strikes Back: Blockbuster's CEO Responds to Icahn's Attacks," *Seeking Alpha.com*, April 18, 2005.

56 Peers, Martin and Zimmerman, Ann, "Dissident Investor Icahn Wins Board Seats at Blockbuster," *Wall Street Journal*, May 12, 2005.

57 Cauthen, Shawn, Director, Keating, Gina, Writer, *Netflix vs. the World*, Documentary Film, 2019.

58 Randolph, Marc, 2019, *That Will Never Work*, Little, Brown and Company, 301-303.

59 Strahlberg, David, "Antioco Strikes Back: Blockbuster's CEO Responds to Icahn's Attacks," *Seeking Alpha.com*, April 18, 2005.

60 Carr, Austin, "Blockbuster CEO Jim Keyes on Bankruptcy, Netflix, and Becoming the Next Apple," FastCompany.com, June 21, 2010.

61 Cauthen, Shawn, Director, Keating, Gina, Writer, *Netflix vs. the World*, Documentary Film, 2019.

62 Boorstin, Julia, "Blockbuster Posts Another Loss Despite Progress," *CNBC.com*, Aug 8, 2008.

63 Schiffman, Betsy, "Blockbuster CEO 'Confused by Fascination' With Netflix," *Wired.com*, Aug 18, 2008.

64 Dowd, Maureen, "Reed Hastings Had Us All Staying Home Before We Had To," *The New York Times*, September 4, 2020.

65 "Land of the Giants: The Netflix Effect, Who Really Killed Blockbuster Video?" *podcasts.apple.com,* June 30, 2020.

66 Farrell, Mike, "Ergen's Blockbuster Victory, *Multichannel.com,* March 29, 2018.

Made in the USA
Middletown, DE
27 May 2023

31588208R00161